For Leon and Oren
with lots of love
Grandad and Nenna

2020

HEATH ROBINSON

Wonderful Contraptions & Extraordinary Inventions

D1555832

AMBERLEY

First published 2015

Amberley Publishing
The Hill, Stroud
Gloucestershire, GL5 4EP

www.amberley-books.com

British Library Cataloguing in Publication Data.
A catalogue record for this book is available from the British Library.

ISBN 978 1 4456 4593 3 (print)
ISBN 978 1 4456 4599 5 (ebook)

Typesetting and Origination by Amberley Publishing.
Printed in the UK.

Contents

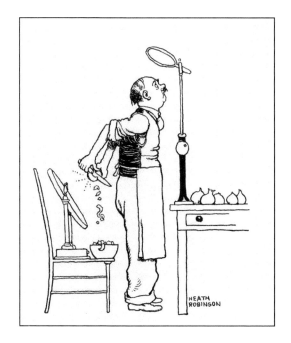

How to avoid tears when peeling onions.

Introduction

The British obsession with gadgetry goes back a very long way, and it is largely due to William Heath Robinson. He was born in the late Victorian age, amid the rise of the industrial landscape and in the heyday of rail travel, and he witnessed both the First and Second World Wars as they pushed technology ever further forward. Perhaps such an era was bound to produce a genius with a love of machines and gizmos. His art remains as funny and relevant as ever today, in a world full of technological devices. Owners of a 'selfie stick' will be astonished to note that Heath Robinson had already anticipated the need for such a contraption (although his solution, involving a pistol, may be marginally less subtle).

The appeal of the Heath Robinson contraption lies in its simplicity. Cogs, levers, bits of string, precarious wooden frames and sometimes a candle or two are all that is necessary to build machines that will make life infinitely easier. The logic is irresistible; Heath Robinson's inventions *should* work, however rickety. They are the obvious answer to all our domestic problems.

Heath Robinson also attempts to assuage some of our curiosity about things that have traditionally happened at work and in factories, away from the eyes of outsiders and jealously guarded against competitors. We have always wanted to know just how soup is ox-tailed, how lemonade is pressed and how artificial teeth are tested; these trade secrets are divulged in full, and never again will frustrated cheese-eaters wonder how Gloucester cheeses are doubled.

Finally, some unusual pastimes, diversions and hobbies would be unimaginable without Heath Robinson. While they may not be for everyone, the folding garden, the device for curing a giraffe's sore throat and a machine for hammering square pegs into round holes are all invaluable contributions to society and hold their own fascination for the average reader. These machines make the improbable possible.

The reader may now be wondering how much string is necessary to build their own Heath Robinson machine and eyeing up the nearest clock to see if it will contain enough cogs. Some would argue that this book should discourage such experiments, and even that it should have a large 'DO NOT TRY THIS AT HOME' sign on the cover. Most, however, will feel that there are simply not enough Heath Robinson machines in the world. So why not try them at home? Just don't expect the clock to work again afterwards.

1

Simple Solutions to Everyday Problems

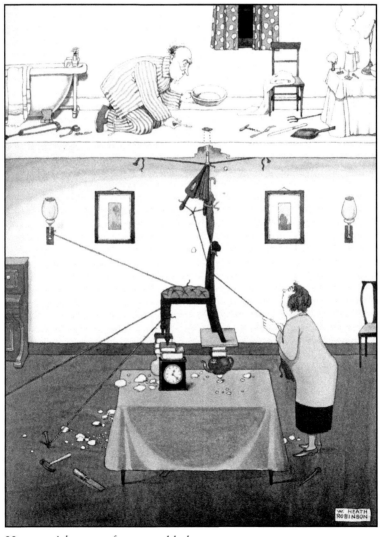

How to pick up a safety razor blade.

The finer points of dancing: An ingenious device which allows the student to learn dancing in his home, and in particular to avoid treading on the toes of his partner.

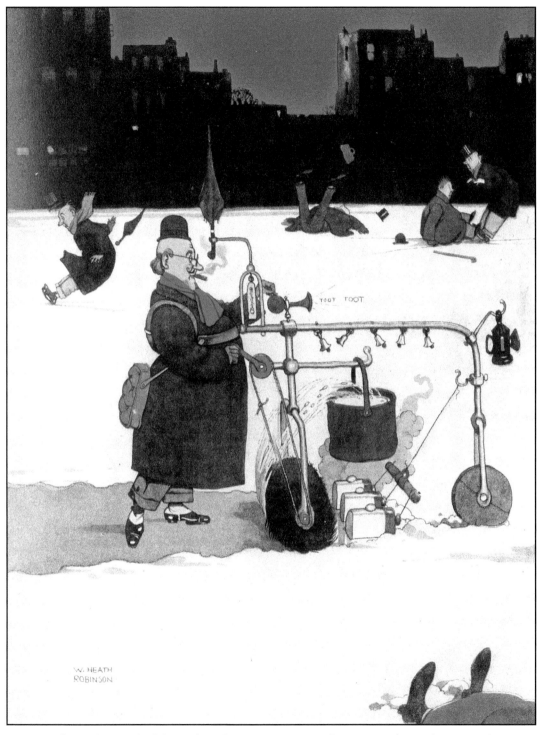

Very hot! The wonderful Heath Robinson new patent thawing machine. This stupendous invention has been specially designed to enable the pedestrian to walk with confidence on the most slippery roads.

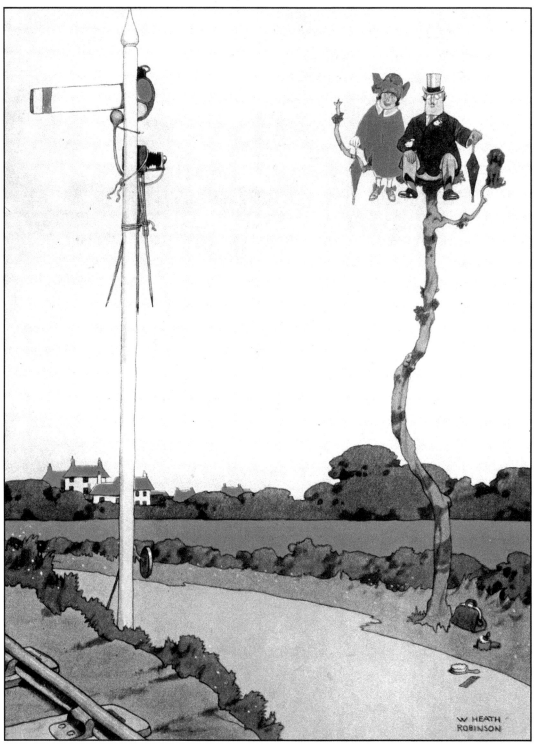

A signal invention: intelligent method of overcoming difficulties of taking one's own photograph.

In the merry, merry spring time: the new Heath Robinson potato dibber for planting seed potatoes in the early spring.

Above: How to obtain a good night's sleep in spite of interruptions.

Opposite: How at last it is possible to keep chickens in the top flat.

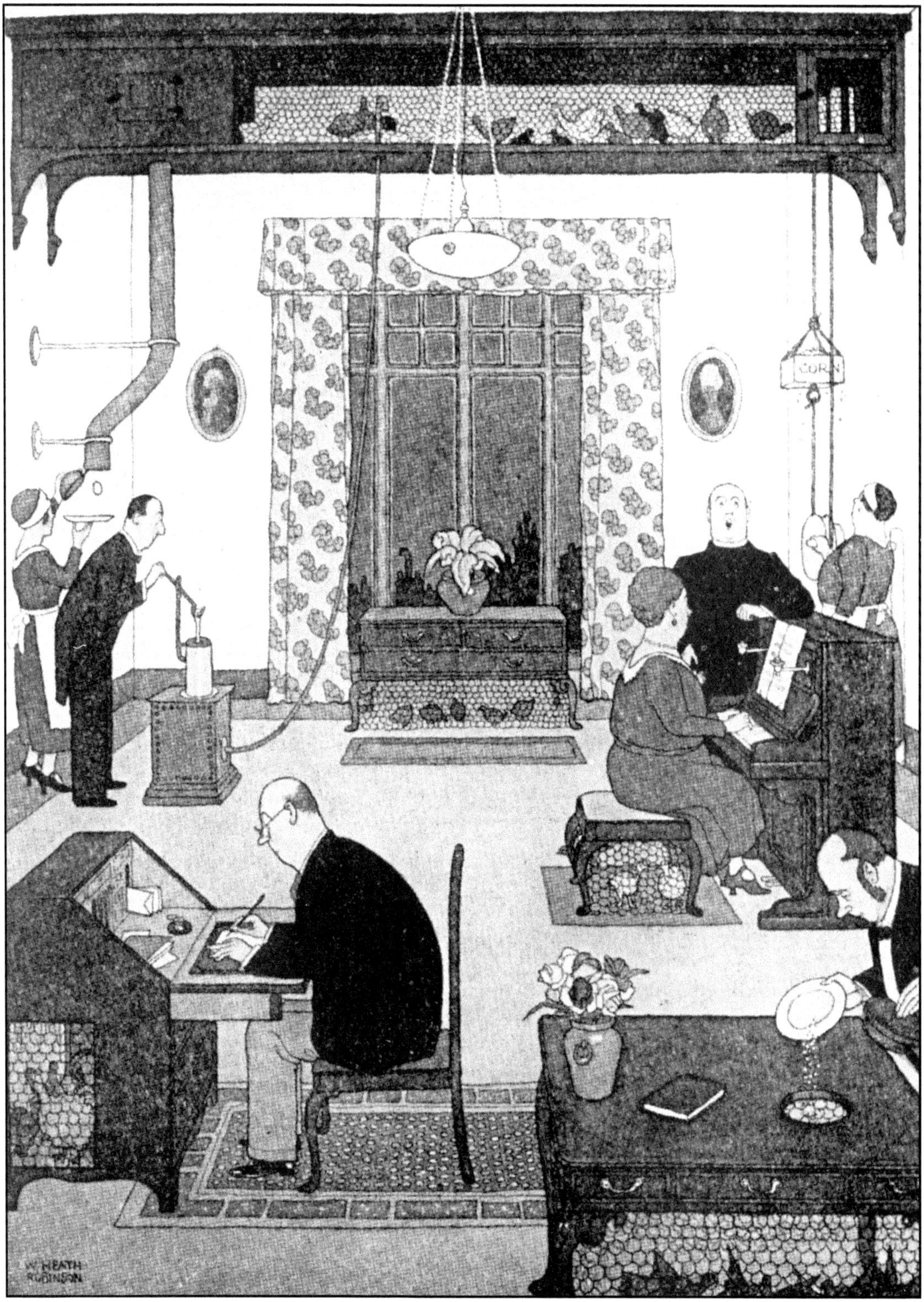
CORN
W. HEATH ROBINSON

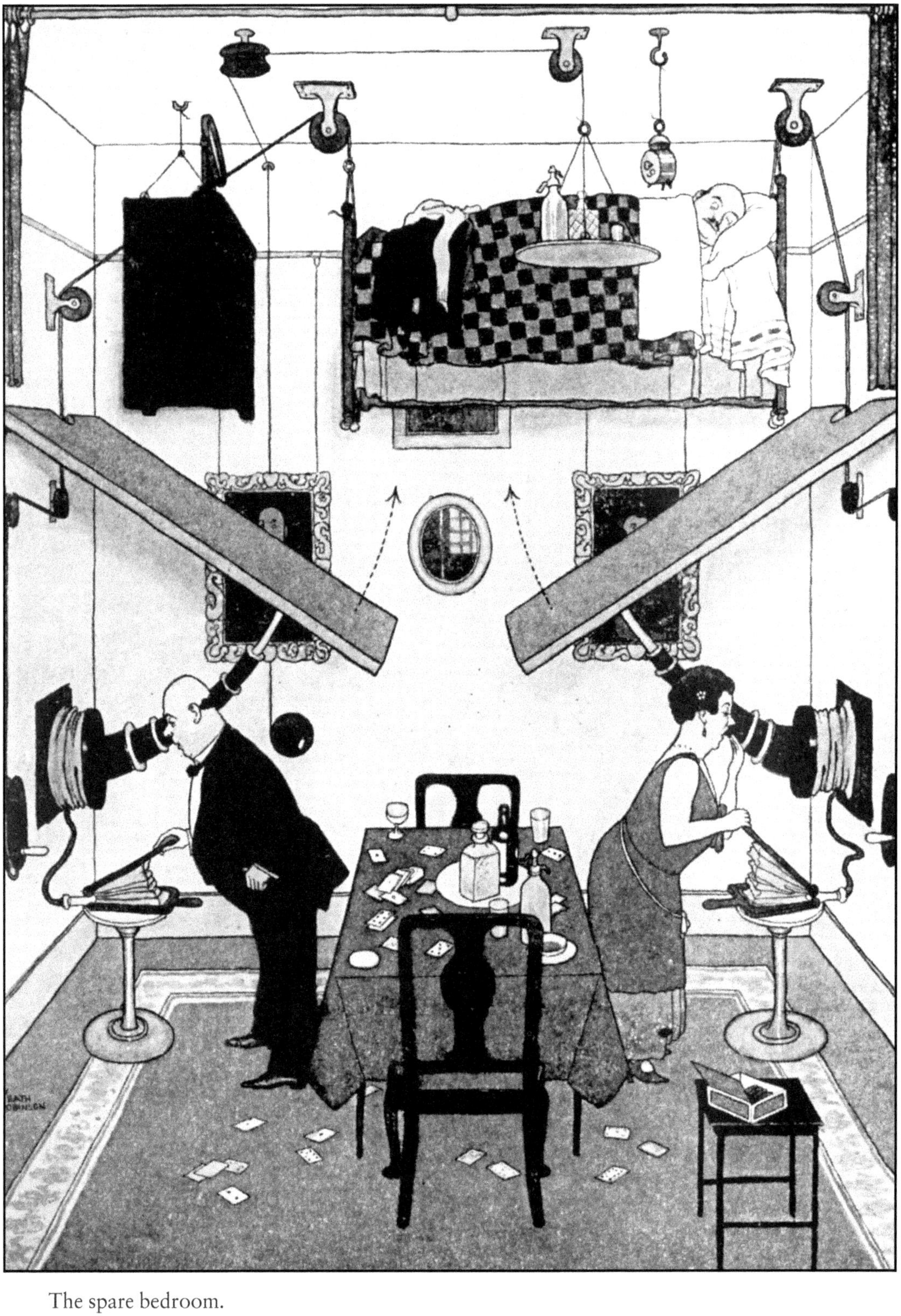

The spare bedroom.

The multi-movement tabby silencer. This apparatus can be operated from the bedroom window and is guaranteed to reach any part of the back yard.

The wart chair. A simple device for removing a wart from the top of the head.

What shall I put on? Bedside contrivance for the changeable season, to indicate the state of the weather and what you should wear when you get up in the morning.

A stormy night at the listening inn. A hitherto unrecorded incidence of a building being saved by wireless during an equinoctial gale.

Up the Bole. Curious disguise assumed by wireless enthusiast to escape payment of his licence.

An out and out success: a remarkable instance of a form of self-dentistry practised by thrifty business-men.

An attractive idea for gents' wear: do you realise that the equinoctial gales will soon be blowing in upon us? If so do not forget to buy one of the new patent adjustable magnetic hat guards, for use with any style and size of hat.

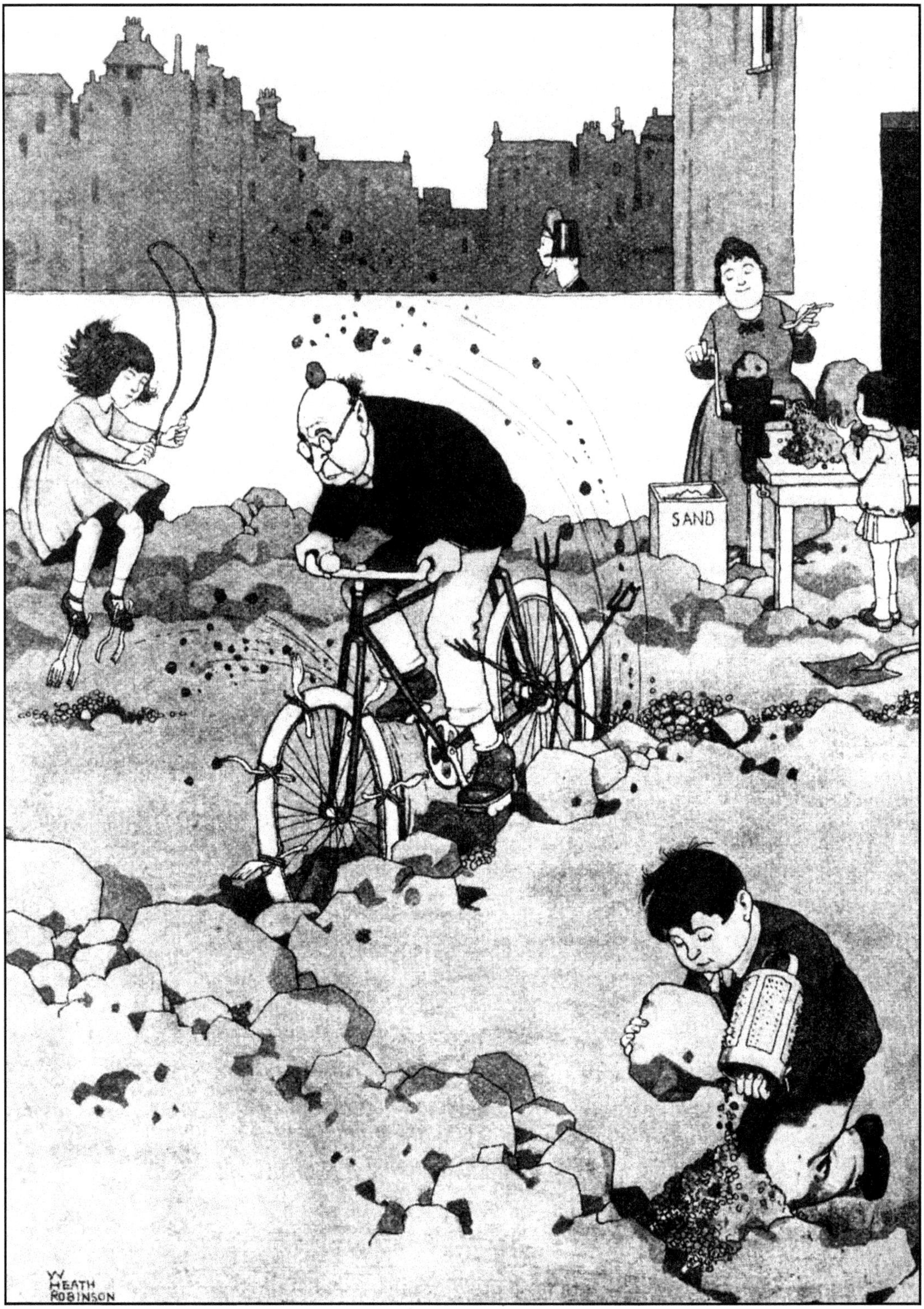
SAND
W HEATH ROBINSON

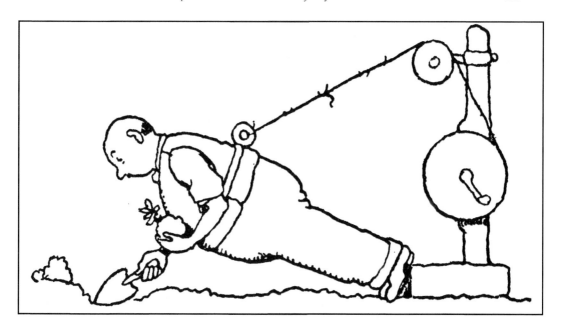

Above: Device for the prevention of gardener's backache.

Opposite: New methods of lightening a heavy soil.

The Eeziweeda, for weeding the garden without treading on the beds.

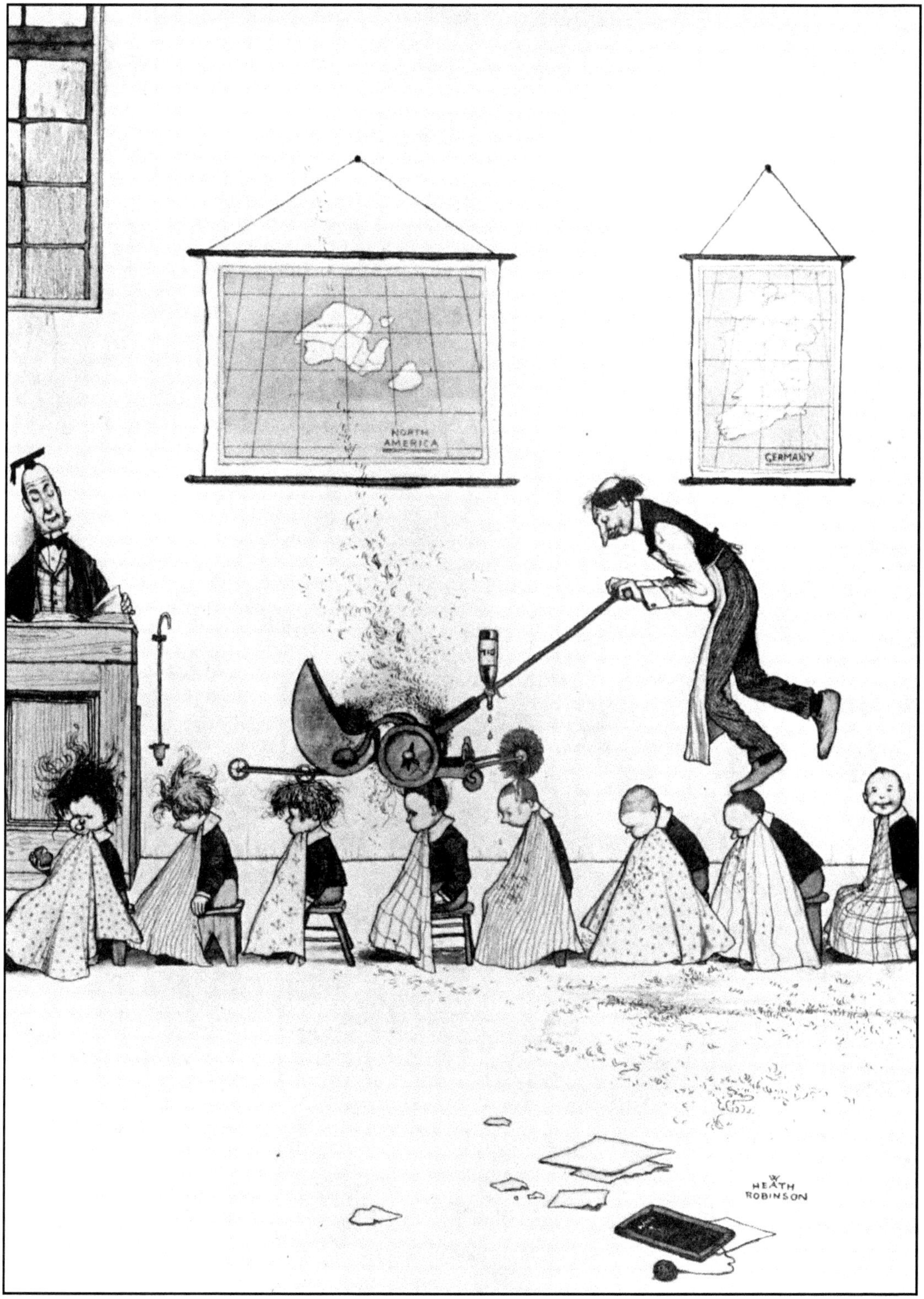
NORTH AMERICA
GERMANY
W HEATH ROBINSON

Hair-cutting day.

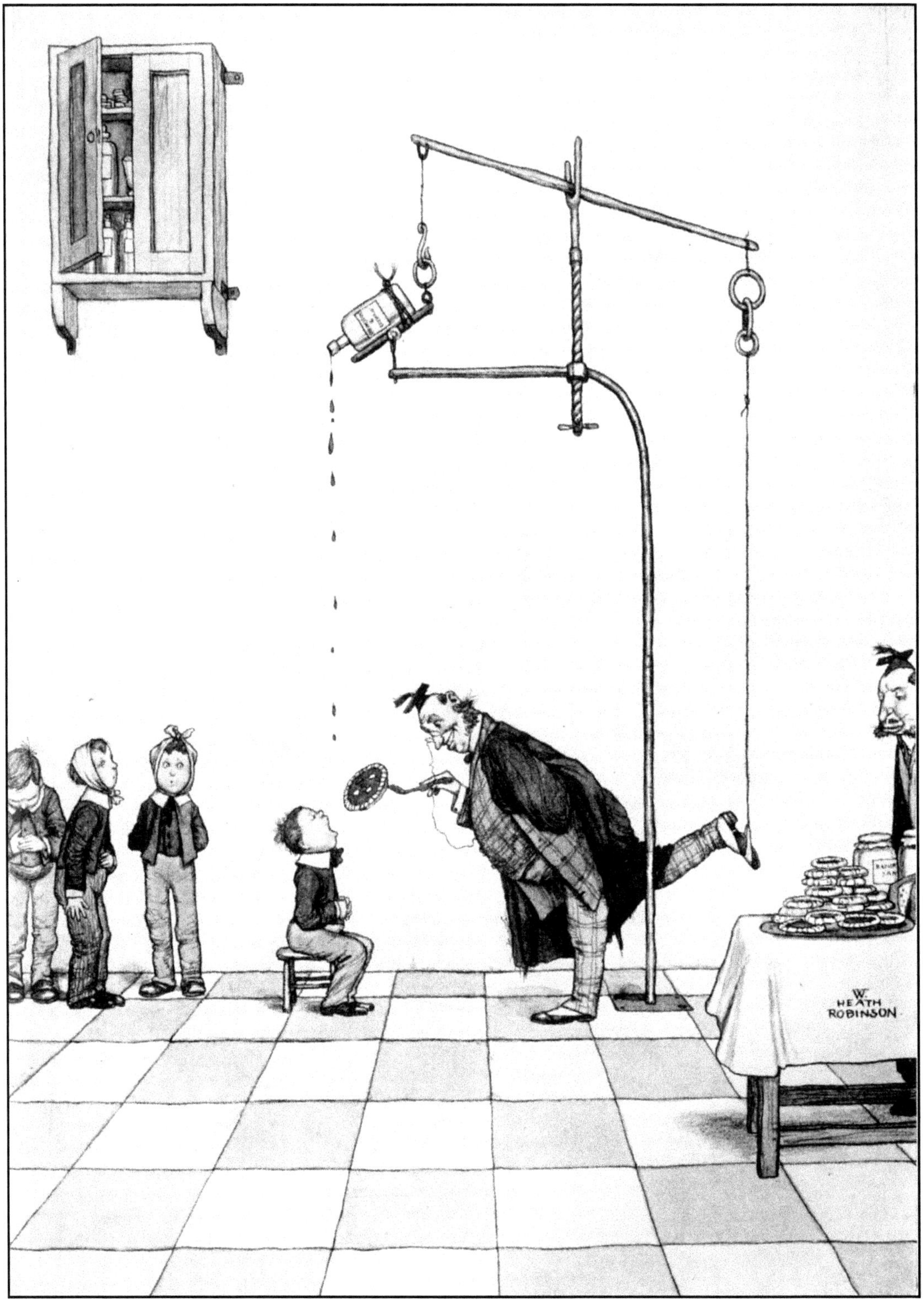
W. HEATH ROBINSON

Medicine morning.

When the hot water tap runs cold: a new device for making a lot out of a little.

Aero-chimney-cleaning: the brainwave of an ex-captain of the RAF (Balloon Section).

Would you be beautiful? A few suggestions for the plain by a well-known beauty specialist.

Doing away with servants in the kitchen.

Doing away with servants in the dining room.

Doing away with servants in the bedroom.

Doing away with servants in the drawing room.

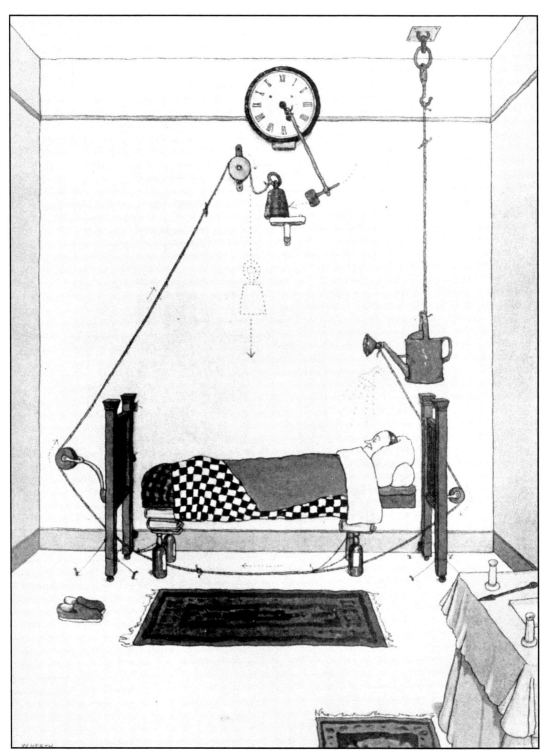

A matter of the moment: a simple expedient to accustom oneself to earlier rising in view of the near approach of summer time.

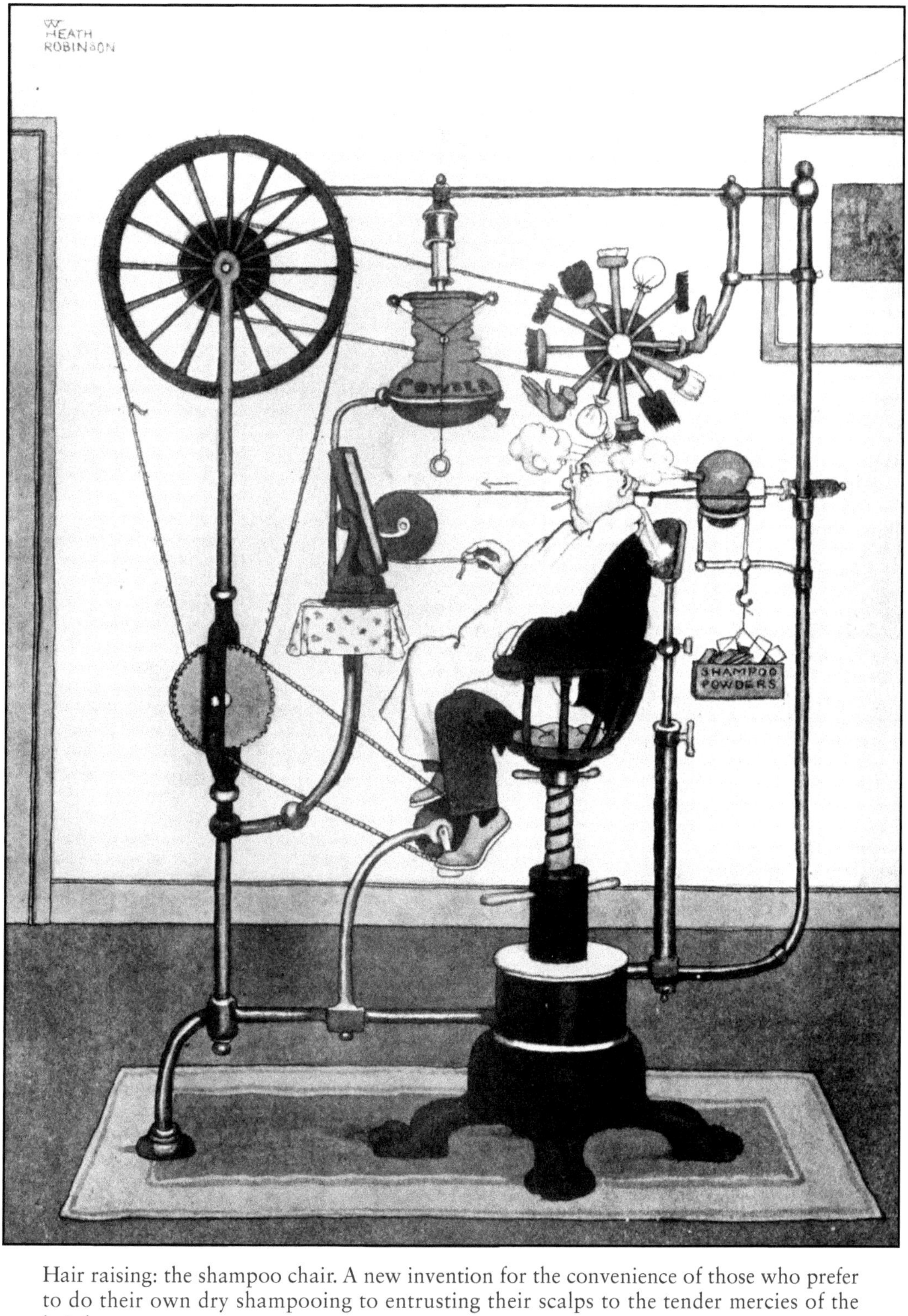
W HEATH ROBINSON
SHAMPOO POWDERS

Hair raising: the shampoo chair. A new invention for the convenience of those who prefer to do their own dry shampooing to entrusting their scalps to the tender mercies of the hairdresser.

'Sleep, my pretty one, sleep!' How one of the many enquiring minds who wonder what they look like when asleep satisfied his curiosity.

Sandpaper chute for removing the shine from blue serge trousers.

Pea eating extraordinary. An elegant and interesting apparatus designed to overcome once and for all the difficulties of conveying green peas to the mouth.

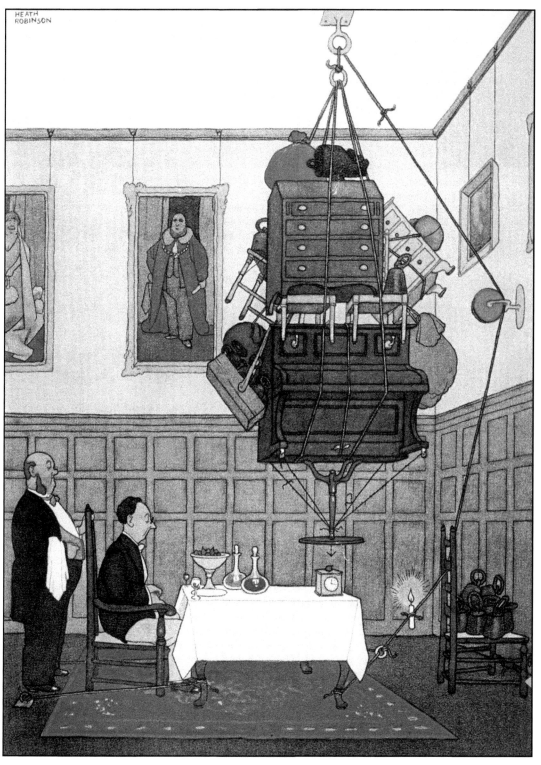

'Everything comes to him who waits.' A simple method of cracking nuts.

'Two's company, three's none.' Sensible precaution against sudden interruption of confidential conversation.

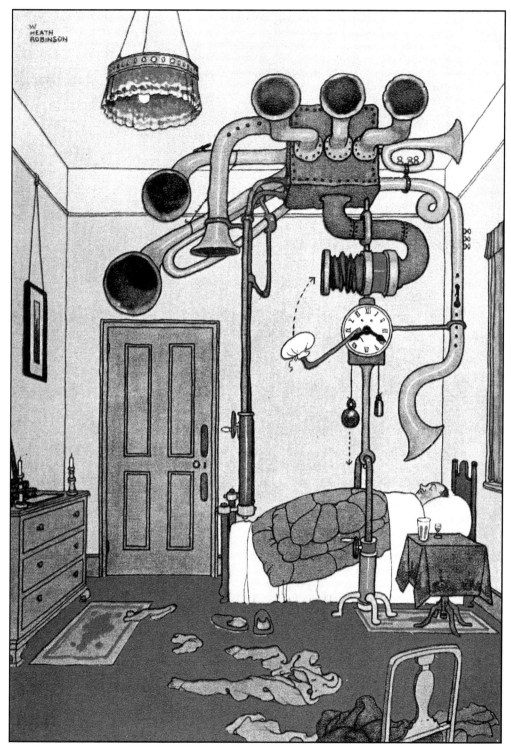

'Early to bed and early to rise, etc., etc.' An ingenious device for getting up in good time in the morning.

Why are people disagreeable at breakfast time?

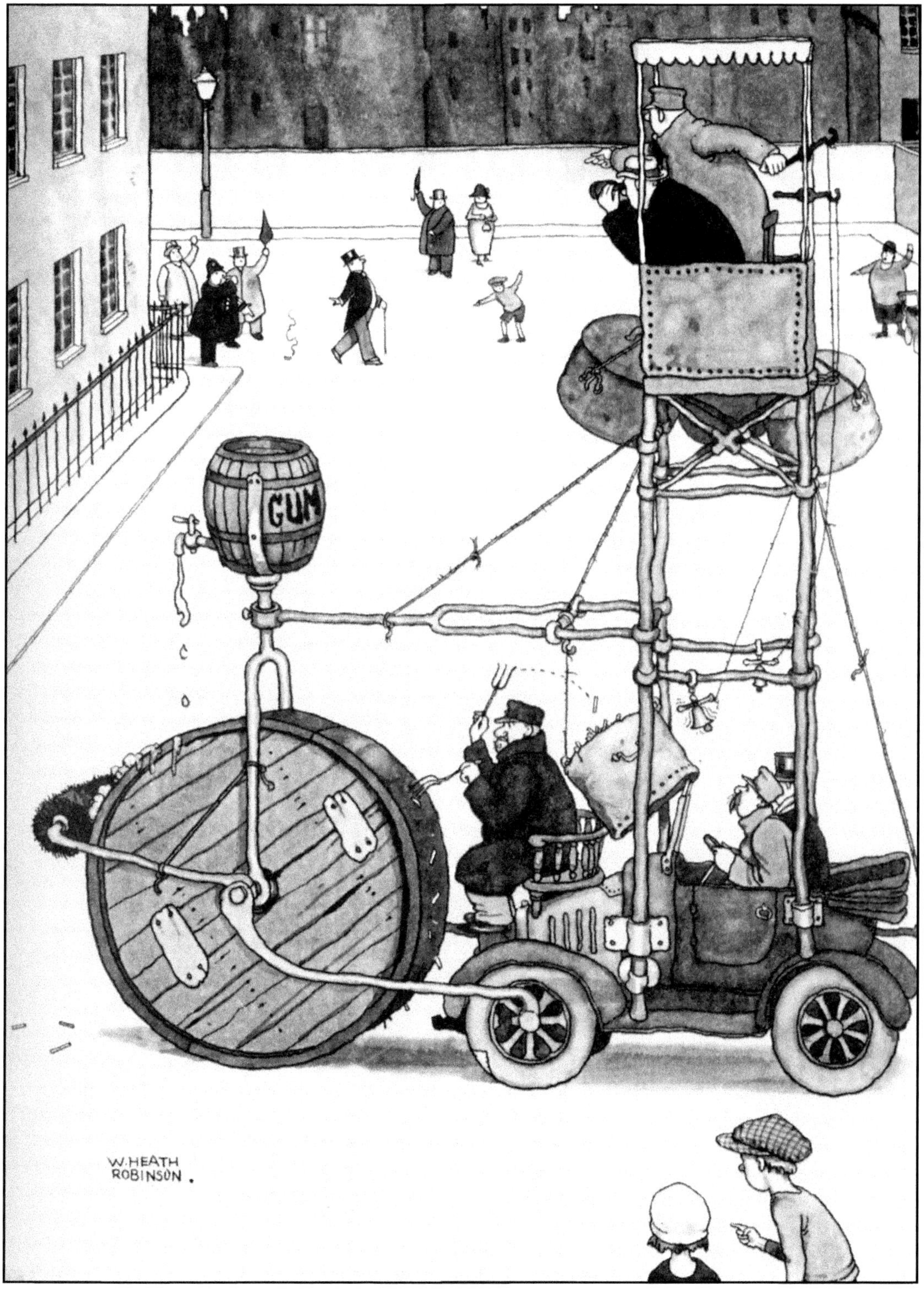
GUM
W. HEATH
ROBINSON

Anti-litter machine.

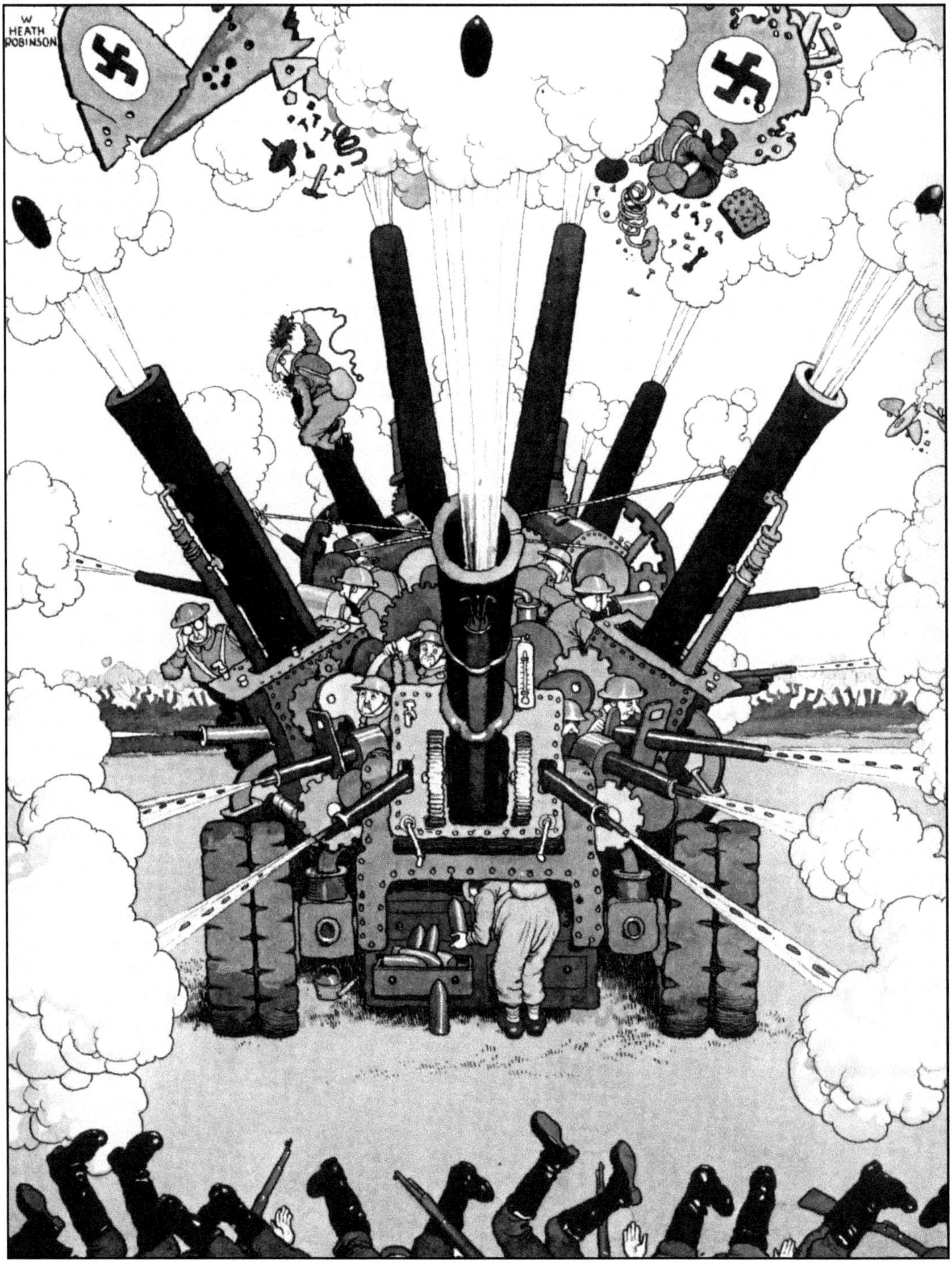
W HEATH ROBINSON

Hit or Missler gun.

Milkman on early morning round.

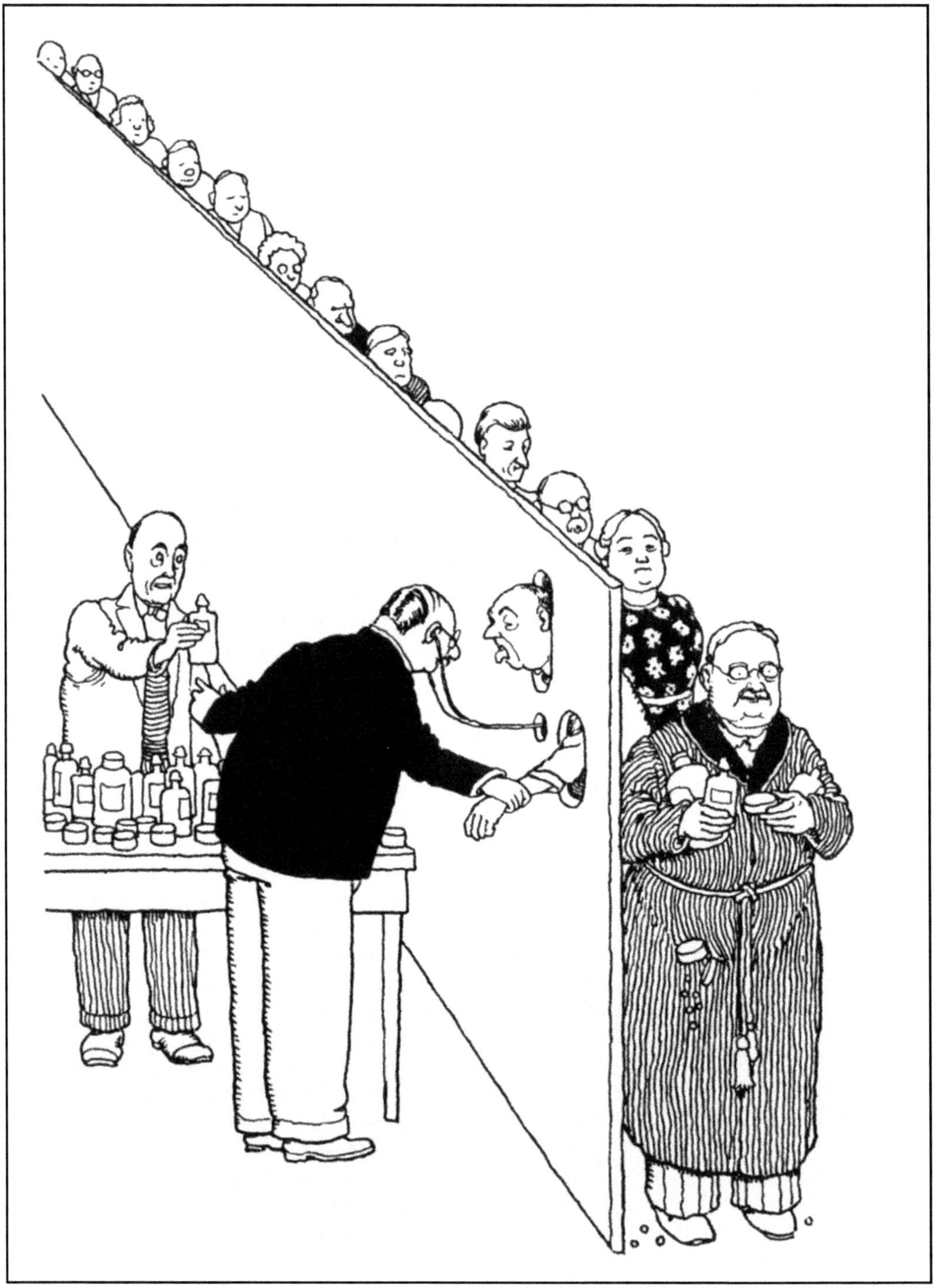

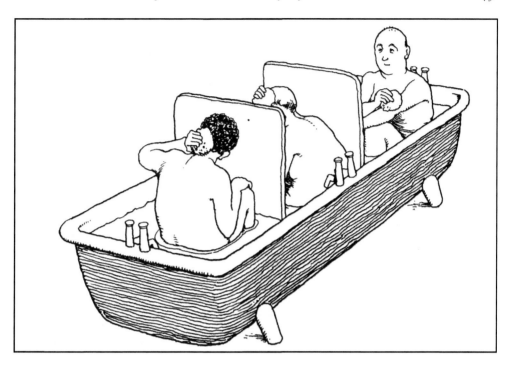

Above: Three-man communal bath.

Opposite: Monthly overhaul.

Six-tier communal cradle.

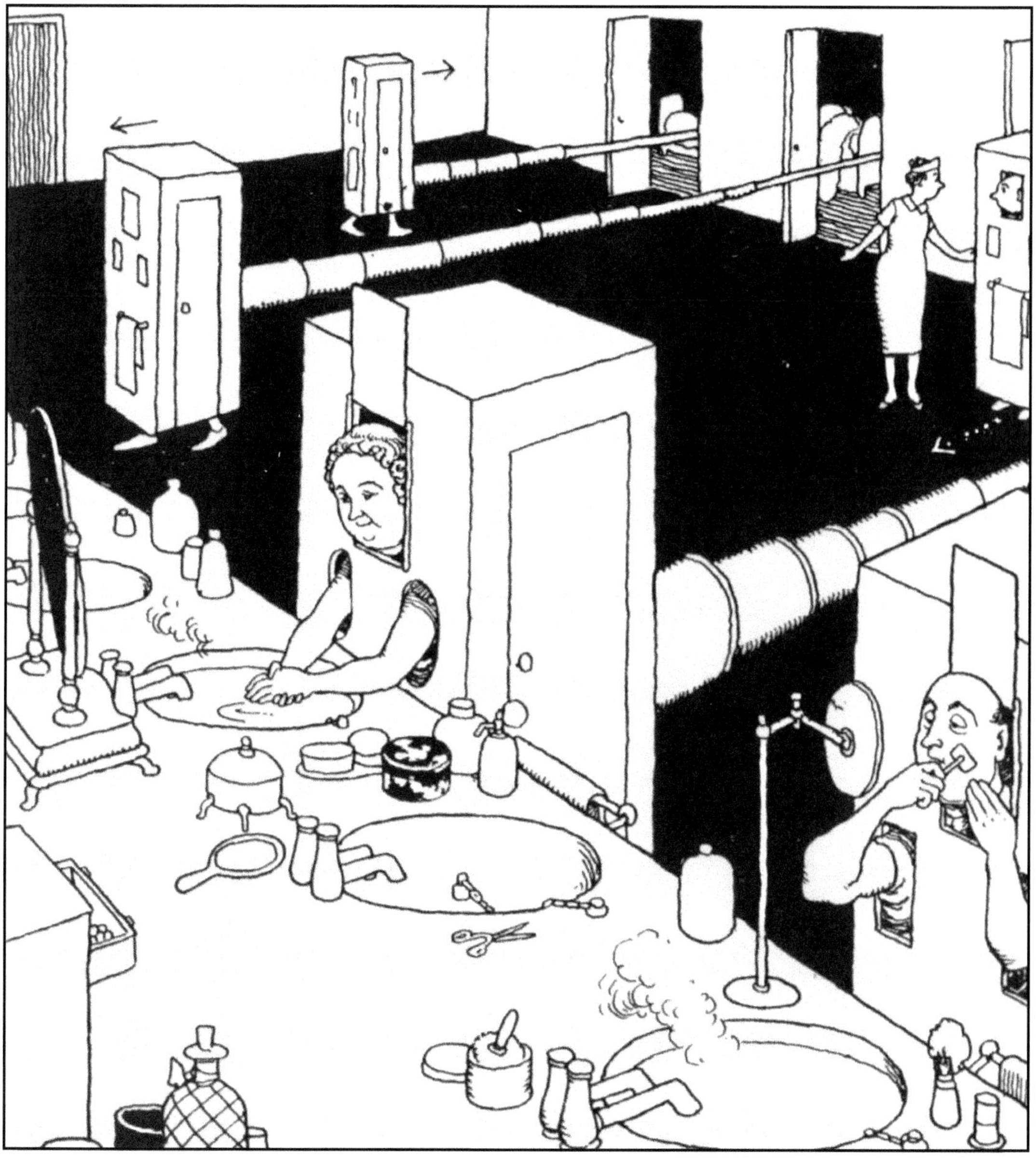

Modesty toilet boxes.

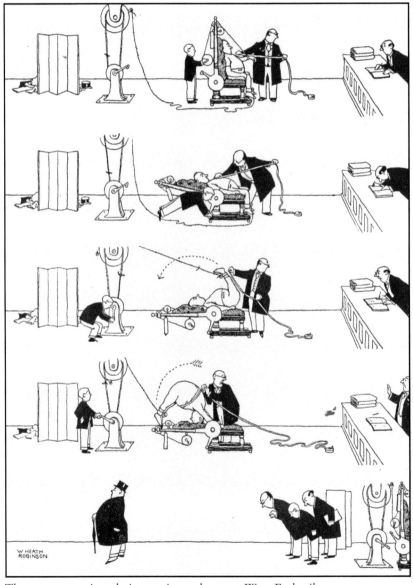

The new measuring-chair now in use by most West-End tailors.

A busy morning in the sumptuous studio of a fashionable hair artist.

How they put the tartans on the kilts in an old kilt-works in the highlands.

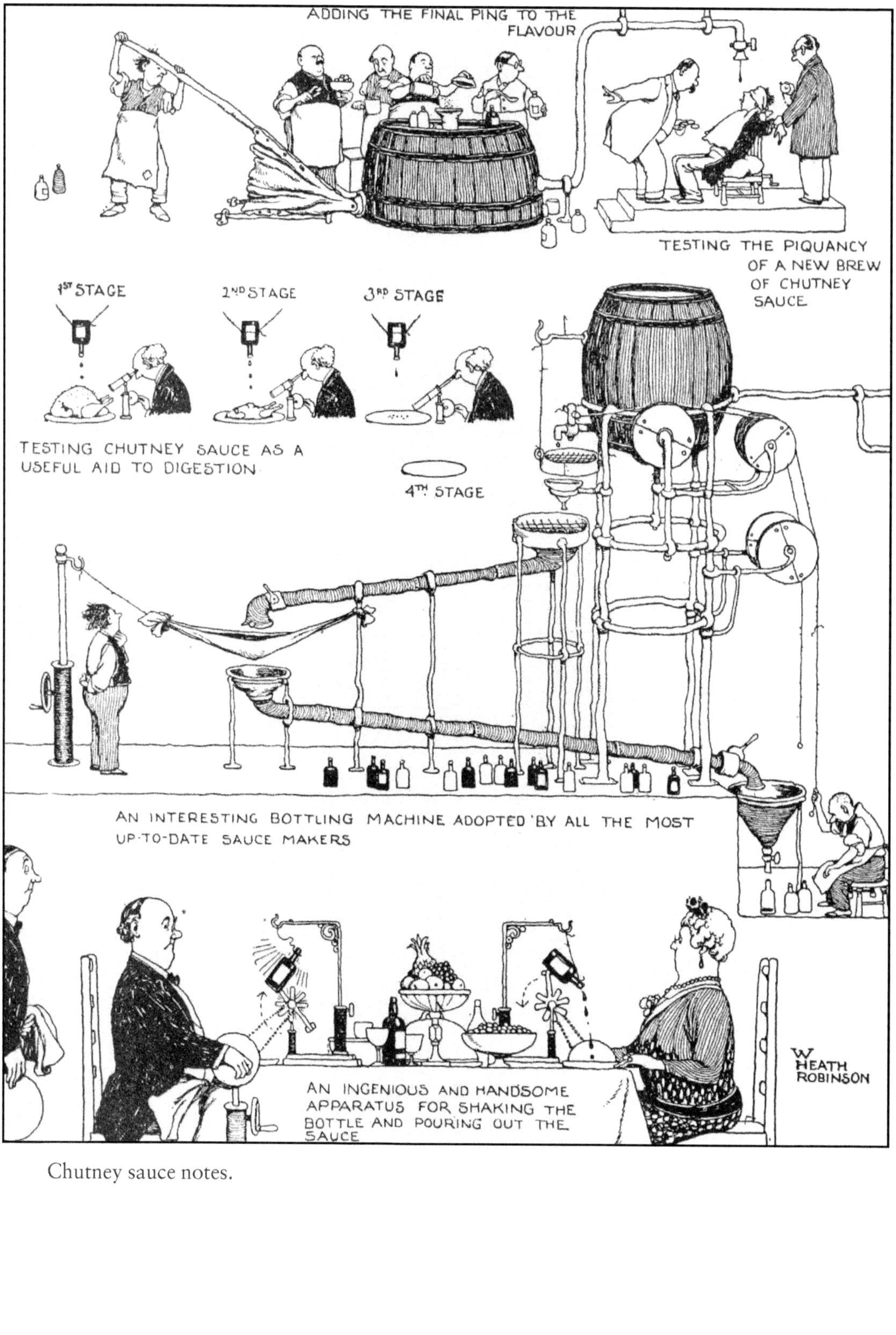
ADDING THE FINAL PING TO THE FLAVOUR
TESTING THE PIQUANCY OF A NEW BREW OF CHUTNEY SAUCE
1ST STAGE
2ND STAGE
3RD STAGE
4TH STAGE
TESTING CHUTNEY SAUCE AS A USEFUL AID TO DIGESTION
AN INTERESTING BOTTLING MACHINE ADOPTED BY ALL THE MOST UP-TO-DATE SAUCE MAKERS
AN INGENIOUS AND HANDSOME APPARATUS FOR SHAKING THE BOTTLE AND POURING OUT THE SAUCE
W HEATH ROBINSON

Chutney sauce notes.

Testing the waterproof qualities of umbrellas in an up-to-date brolley works.

Interesting treatment of cattle on an Argentine stock farm to make the meat soft and tender before killing.

Half-hours at a mattress-making factory.

Hague Convention defied! The Germans use button magnets.

Kolossal! Krupp's Great Reconnoitring Mortar.

War komforts! Some notes in a German bivouac.

British patent (applied for). The Lancing Wheel for teaching young lancers to lance.

Frightfulness! Germans training wasps to sting Highlanders in Flanders.

Palming themselves off! British soldiers disguised as a palm grove upsetting an enemy bivouac.

The broadcast play. How they make the sound effects.

Kippering herrings by the side of the river Yare.

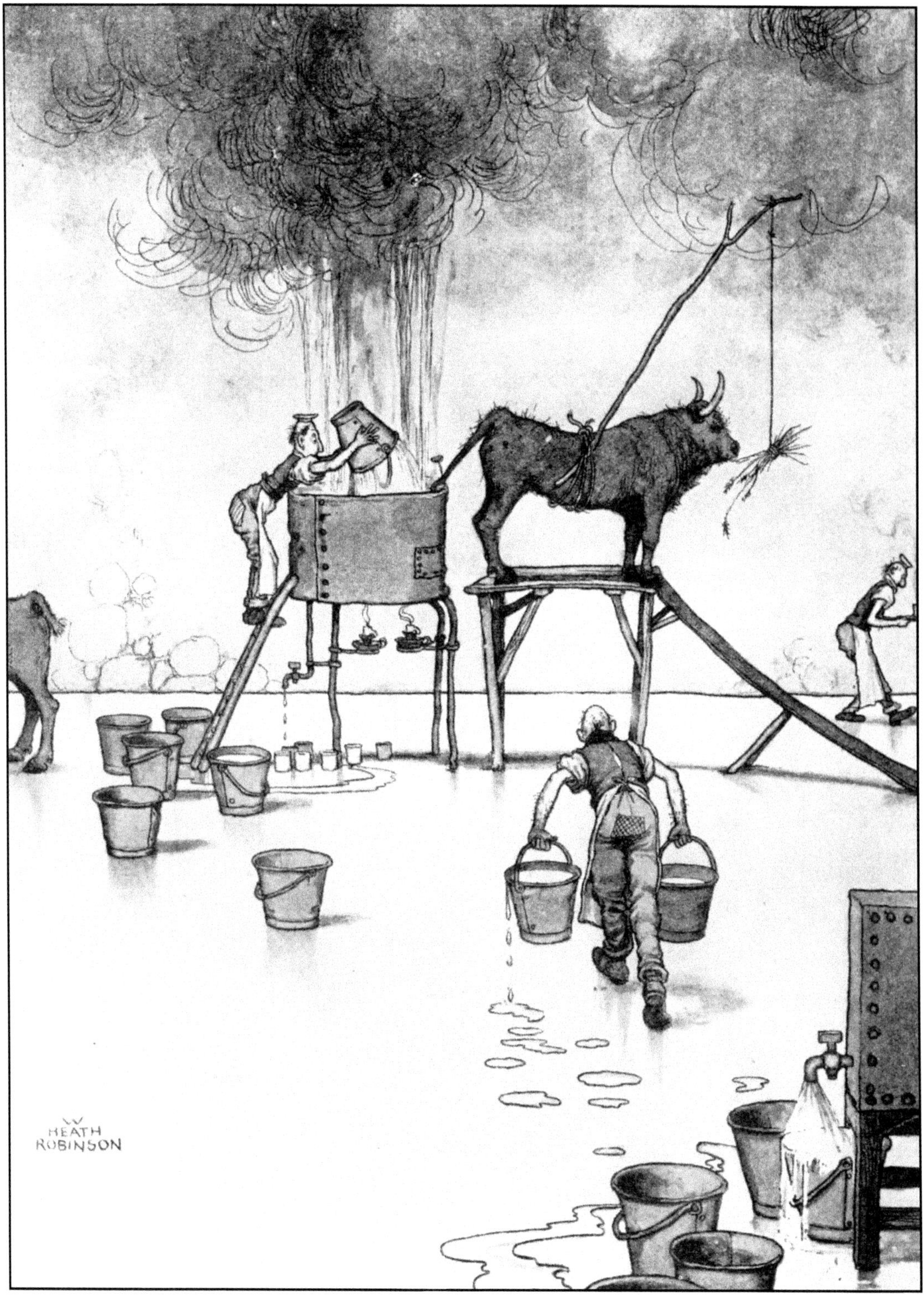
W HEATH ROBINSON

Ox-tailing soup.

Stiltonising cheese in the stockyards of Cheddar.

In the pea-splitting sheds of a soup factory.

The halfpenny testing department of the Mint.

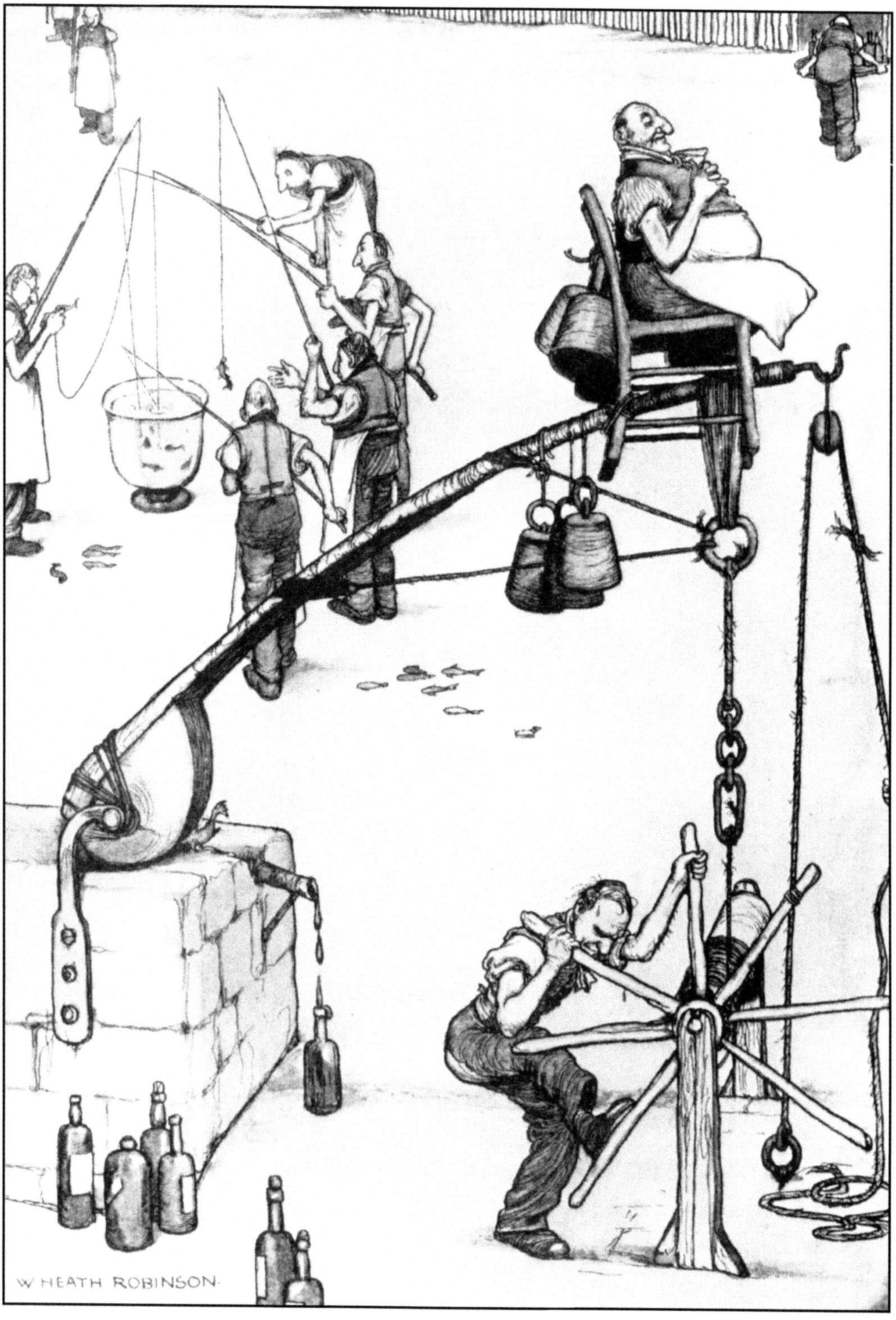
W HEATH ROBINSON

Brewing anchovy sauce.

In the pressing rooms of a lemonade distillery.

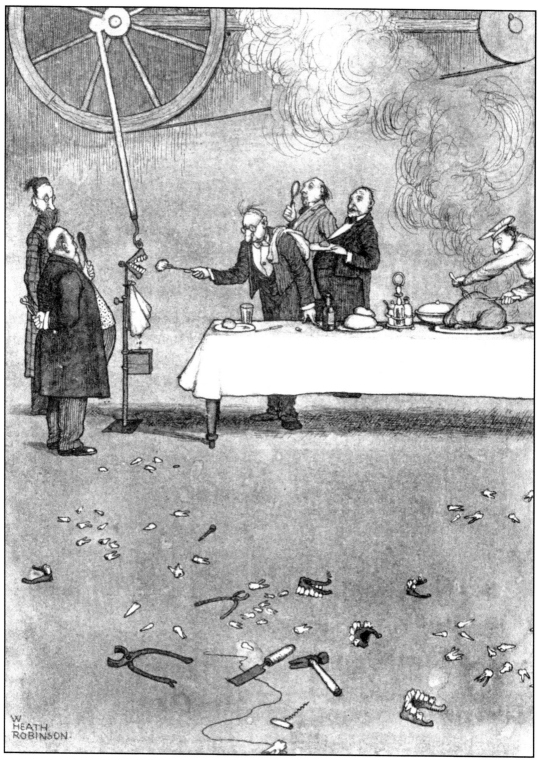

Testing artificial teeth in a dental laboratory.

The editing and production of the sketch – in the editorial department: the editor and some of his staff at work.

Testing candidates – for the post of milk sourer at a cream cheese factory.

Latest machine for tipping matches with phosphorus.

'Our rugged island brace.' Testing the strength of British braces in one of our most important factories in the Midlands.

Weighty deeds afoot – testing corn plasters in the salon of a fashionable West-End chiropodist.

An interesting afternoon with Mr Bryant and Mr May at their famous safety-match works.

Ending in smoke: an ingenious smoke-screen spreader for preventing embarrassing situations when the bathroom lock is out of order.

Testing artificial teeth in a modern tooth works.

The new salmon squeezer fitted with patent filleter.

Sidelights on the wig industry.

A leak in the Channel Tunnel.

Camouflage on Salisbury Plain.

Delayed action bomb machine.

Safe practice for paratrooopers.

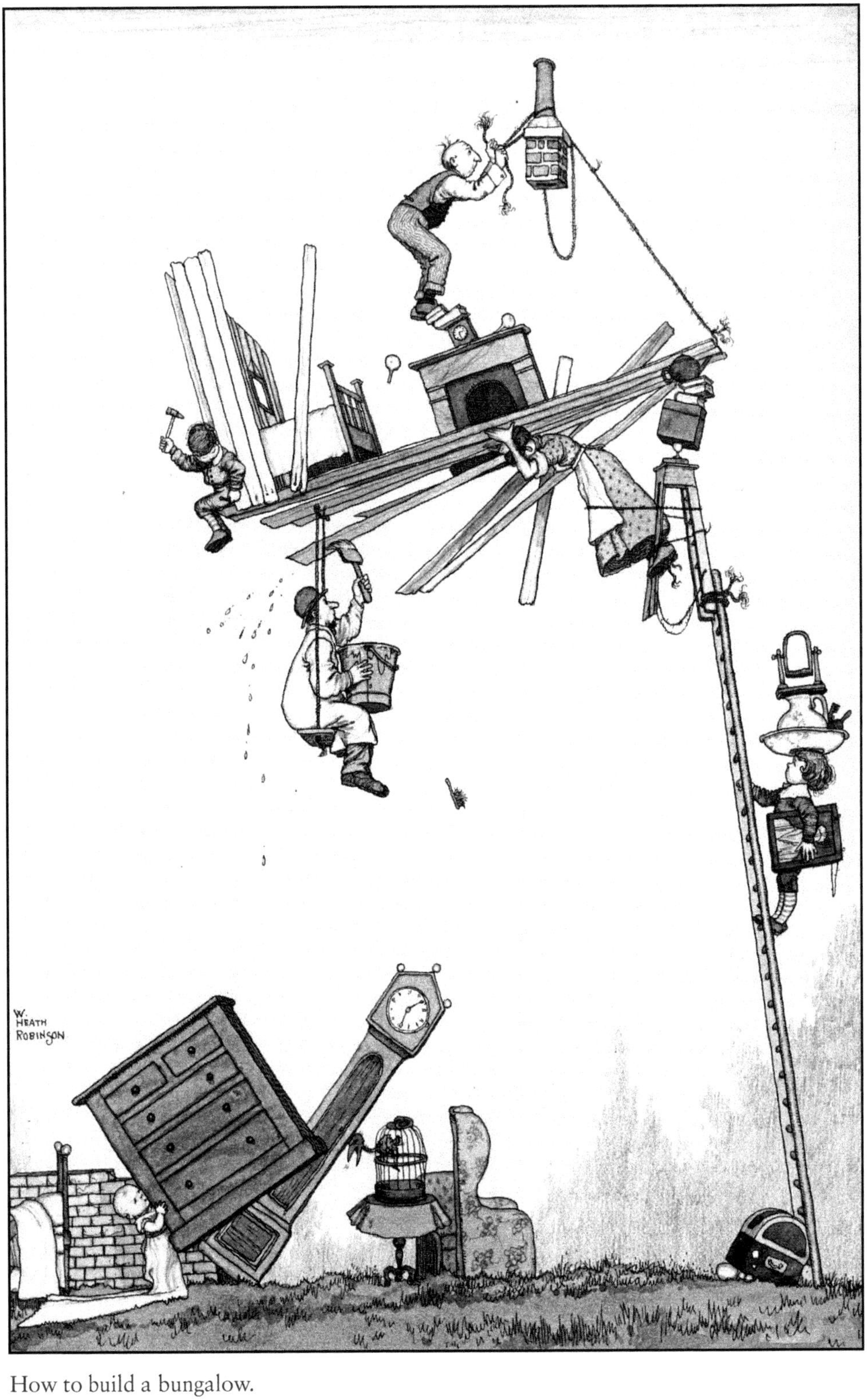
W. HEATH ROBINSON

How to build a bungalow.

Doubling Gloucester cheeses.

The Welsh Rarebit Machine.

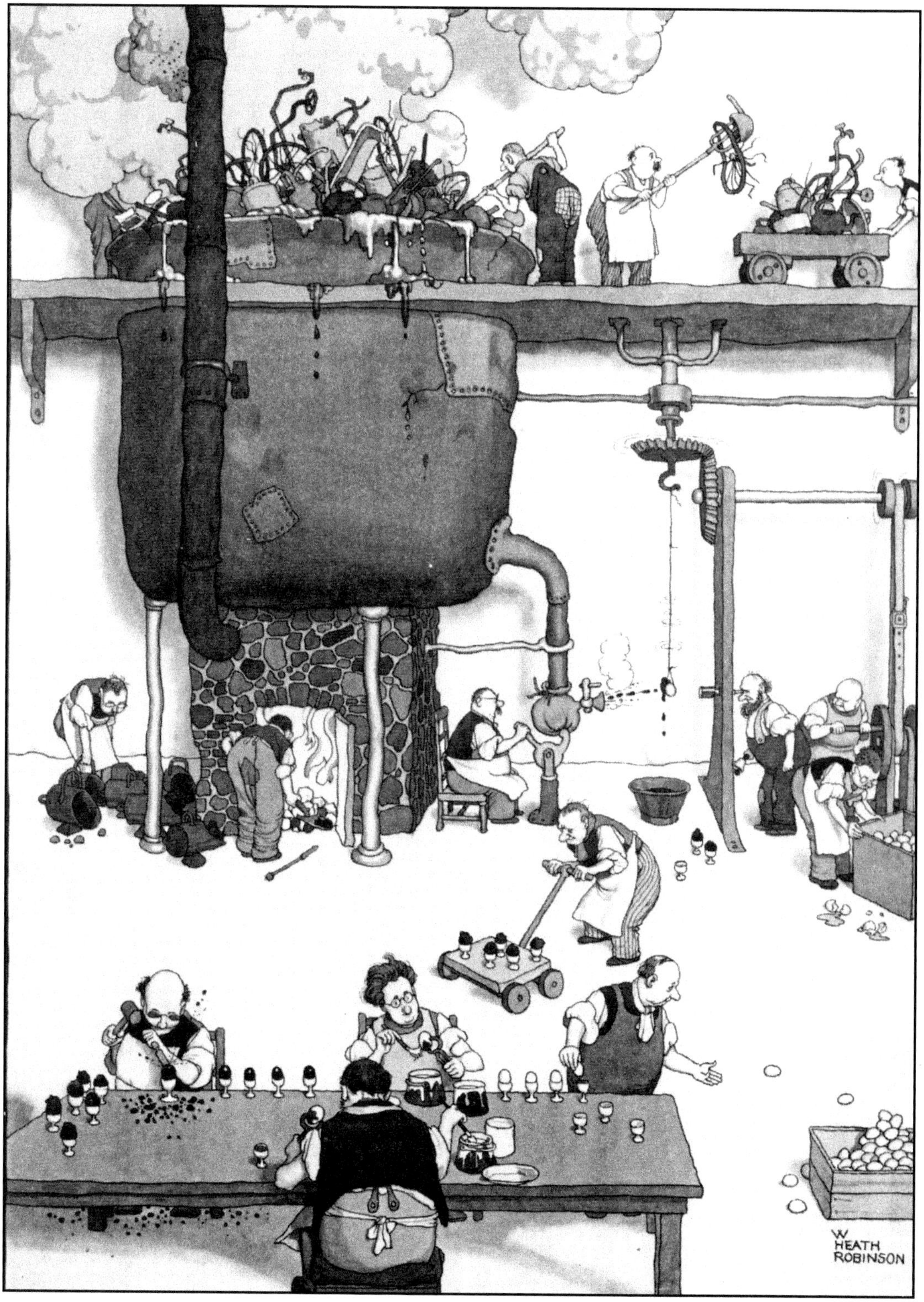
W HEATH ROBINSON

Egg armour plating.

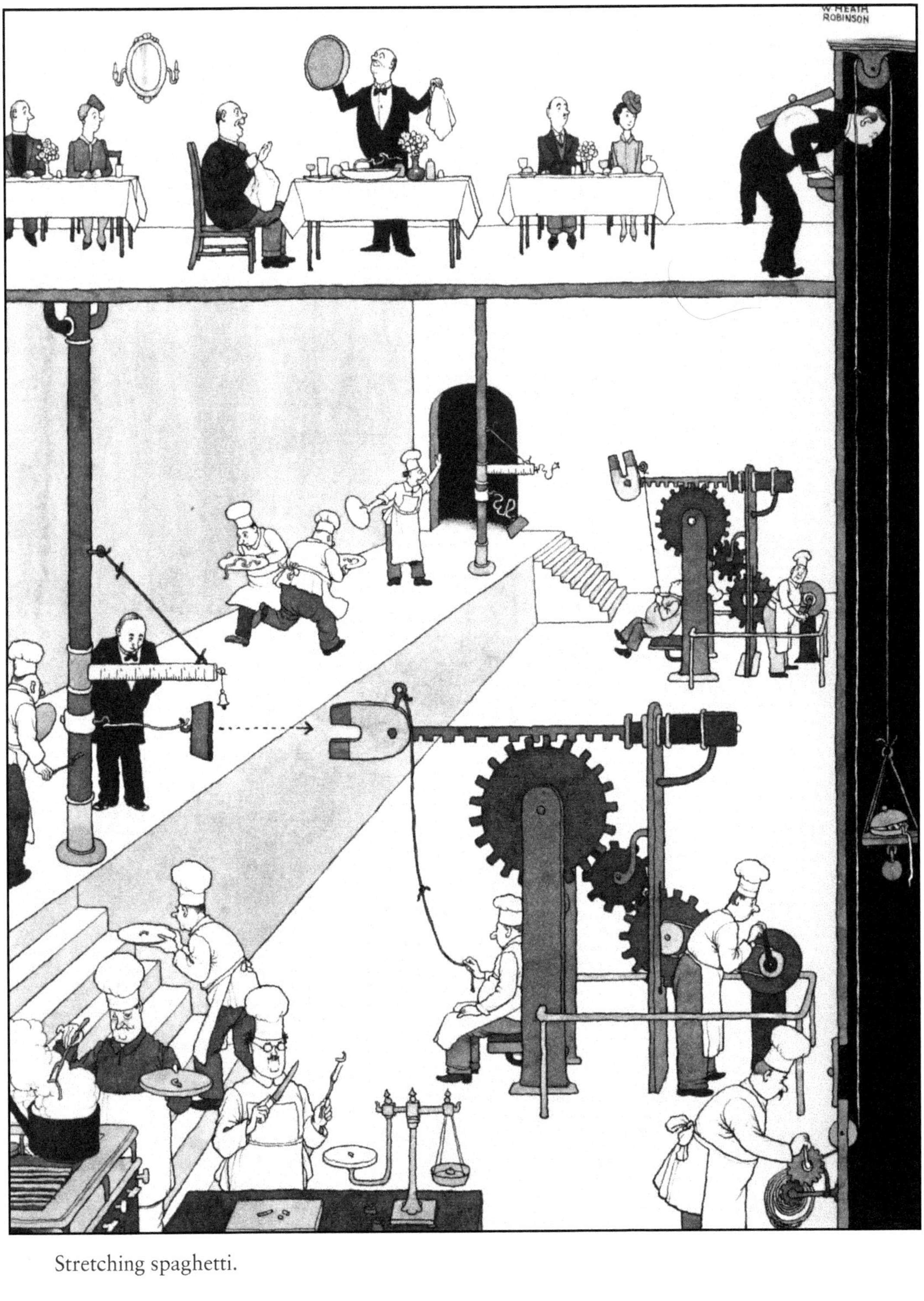
W HEATH
ROBINSON

Stretching spaghetti.

3

Peculiar Pastimes

The soundness of Newton's laws.

666

Heath Robinson Crusoe

Has the whimsical imagination of W. Heath Robinson ever evolved anything more humorous than these illustrations of "Robinson Crusoe" up-to-date?

HIS AEROPLANE.

"AND, IN A WORD, I GOT ALL THIS SAFE ON SHORE ALSO."

His aeroplane.

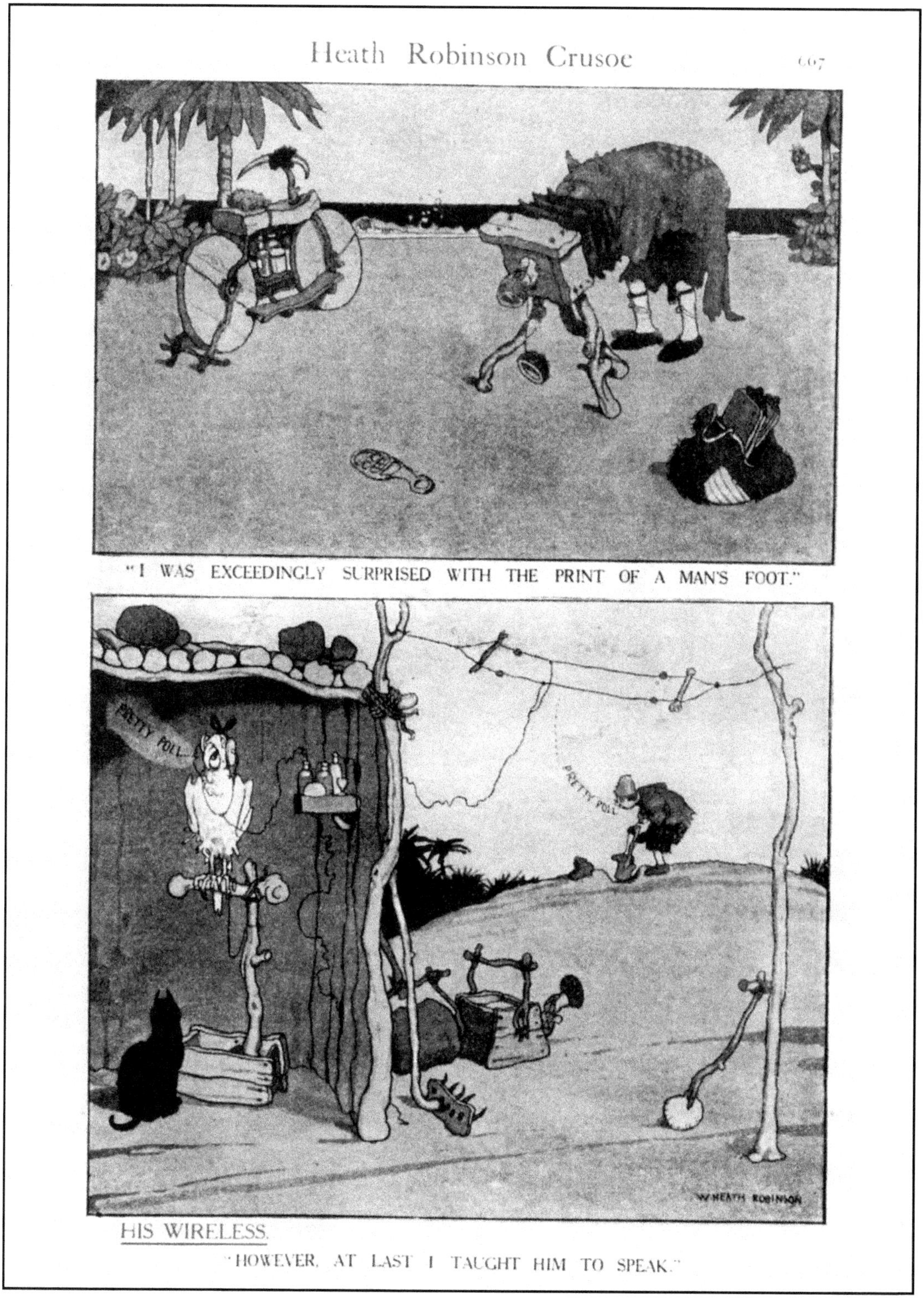
Heath Robinson Crusoe
667
"I WAS EXCEEDINGLY SURPRISED WITH THE PRINT OF A MAN'S FOOT."
PRETTY POLL...
PRETTY POLL
W HEATH ROBINSON
HIS WIRELESS.
"HOWEVER, AT LAST I TAUGHT HIM TO SPEAK."

His wireless.

668   Heath Robinson Crusoe

HIS HOME LIFE.

"IT WAS NOW THAT I BEGAN SENSIBLY TO FEEL HOW MUCH MORE HAPPY
THIS LIFE I NOW LED WAS."

His home life.

Heath Robinson Crusoe

HIS SUBMARINE

"AND THUS I EVERY NOW AND THEN TOOK A LITTLE VOYAGE."

His submarine.

HIS RECREATION.

"I BEGAN NOW TO HAVE SOME USE FOR MY TONGUE AGAIN."

His recreation.

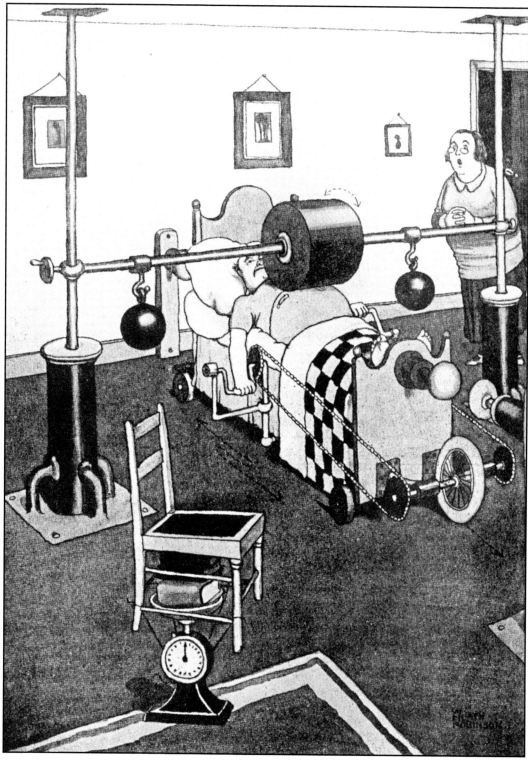

The new banting bed for reducing the figure.

Successful outcome of intelligent precaution observed by old lady in the Sound of Mull.

Remarkable presence of mind of a cinematographer who took and interesting close-up of himself during an accidental fall from the top of Beachy Head.

Resuscitating stale railway scones for redistribution at the station buffets.

Square pegs into round holes.

Munitions! Testing mines at Cuxhaven.

British patent (applied for). A trained dog of war drawing the enemy's fire.

Listening in – that aerial vibration.

Some new wireless tests.

Laudable attempt to cure a giraffe's sore throat, made by a kind-hearted scout.

The new fruit tree pruner with ingenious adjustment for automatically lime-washing the bark while pruning the branches.

The Pilsner Pump for stealing the enemy's supper beer.

From Heath Robinson Unlimited, the world famous manufacturers of 'Glorious Gadgets': some really new Christmas presents.

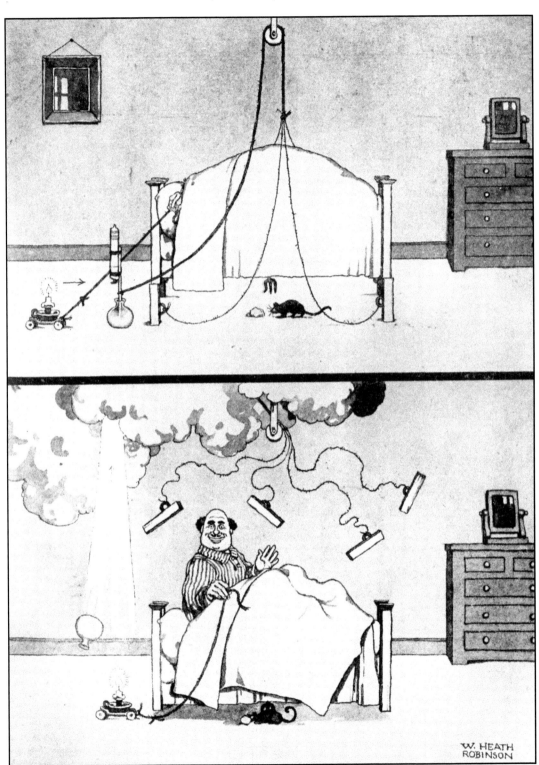

Straight from our Inventions Department: rats – and how to catch them.

Bombing tunny in the lagoons at Bude.

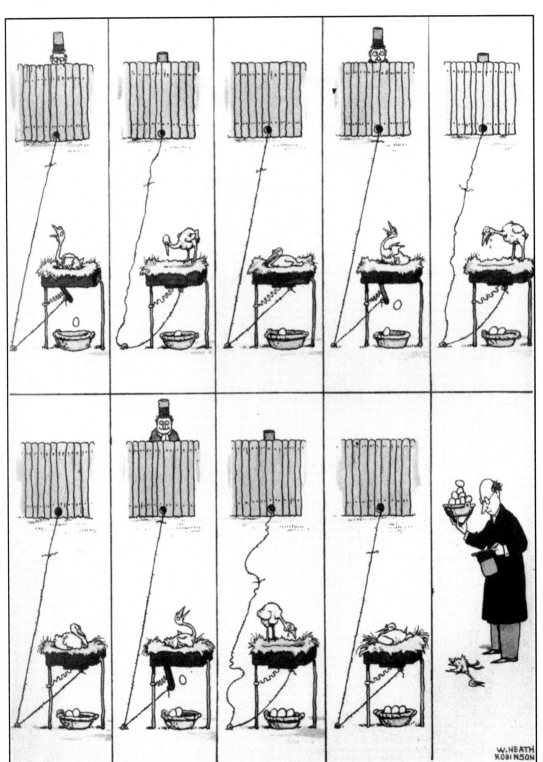

Mass production: forcing eggs for the London market.

For bashful bachelors: the new portable wireless set for delicate propositions. (Beware broadcasting!)

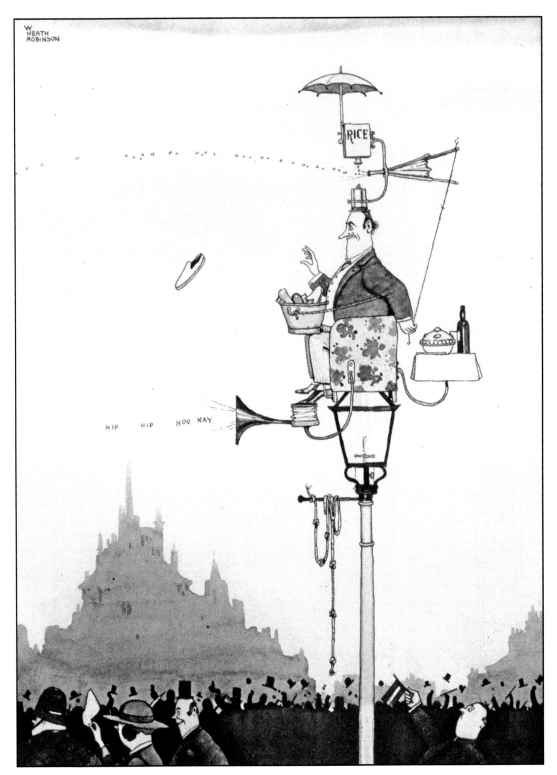

A great grand stand: a comfortable suggestion for viewing future royal weddings.

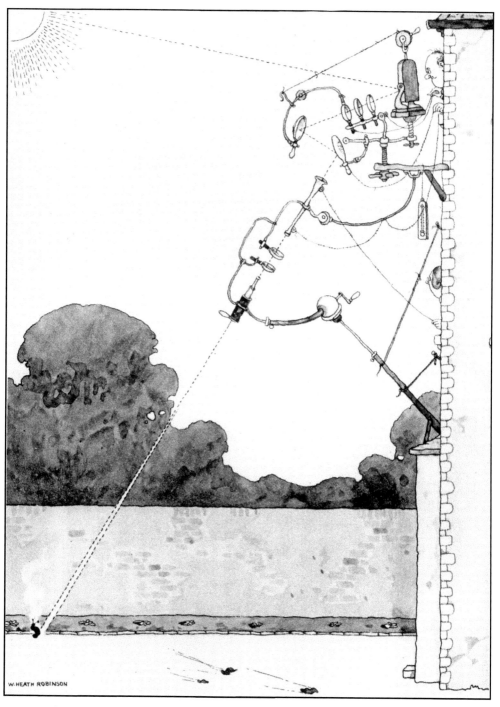

Hurray for the Robinson Ray! We are privileged to publish the first illustration of a Death Ray at its dirty work. The secret experiment was entirely successful and as our picture shows resulted in the slaughter of a slug from a top story window. (NB – The Government is still undecided as to the purchase of Mr HR's patent. Meanwhile, private offers will be considered.)

A moving cat-astrophe: a sectional view of a clever trap by which one of the 'cat' burglars was lured to his doom.

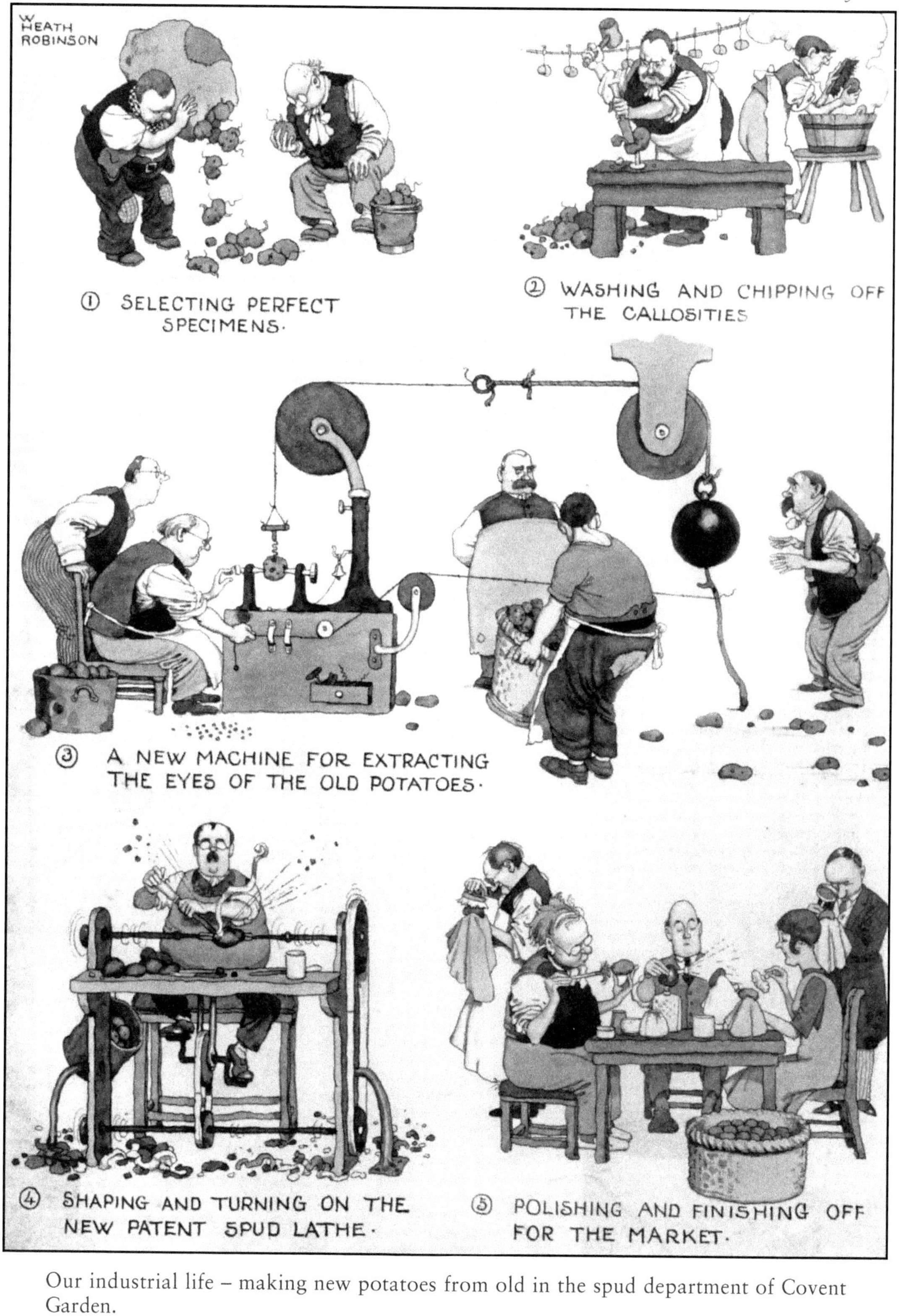
W HEATH ROBINSON
① SELECTING PERFECT SPECIMENS.
② WASHING AND CHIPPING OFF THE CALLOSITIES
③ A NEW MACHINE FOR EXTRACTING THE EYES OF THE OLD POTATOES.
④ SHAPING AND TURNING ON THE NEW PATENT SPUD LATHE.
⑤ POLISHING AND FINISHING OFF FOR THE MARKET.

Our industrial life – making new potatoes from old in the spud department of Covent Garden.

The frame up: one of the new training frames for instructing young cat burglars in the art of overcoming obstacles in their path.

'All's fair in love and war.' A cleverly planned elopement.

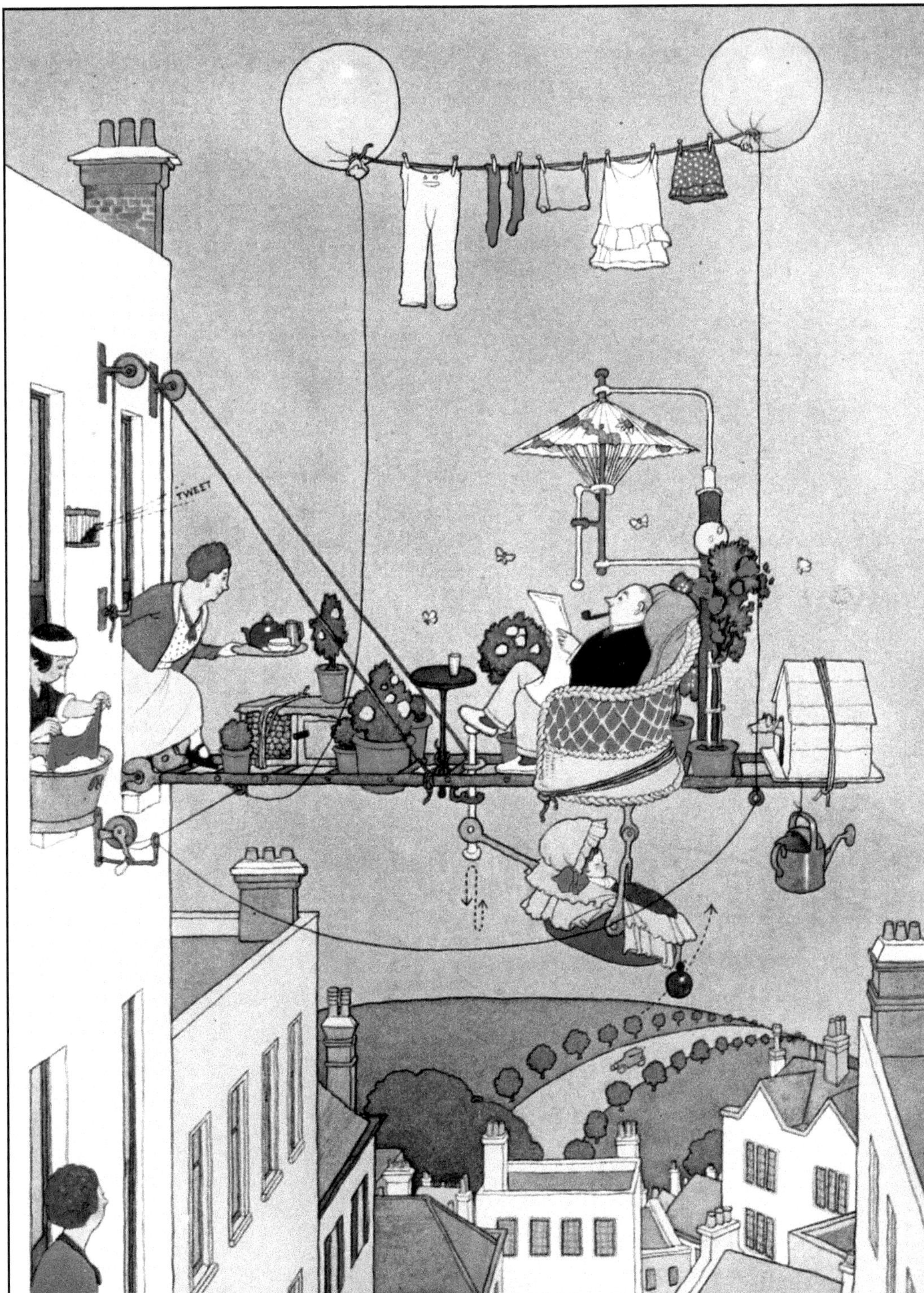
TWEET
W. HEATH ROBINSON

The folding garden.

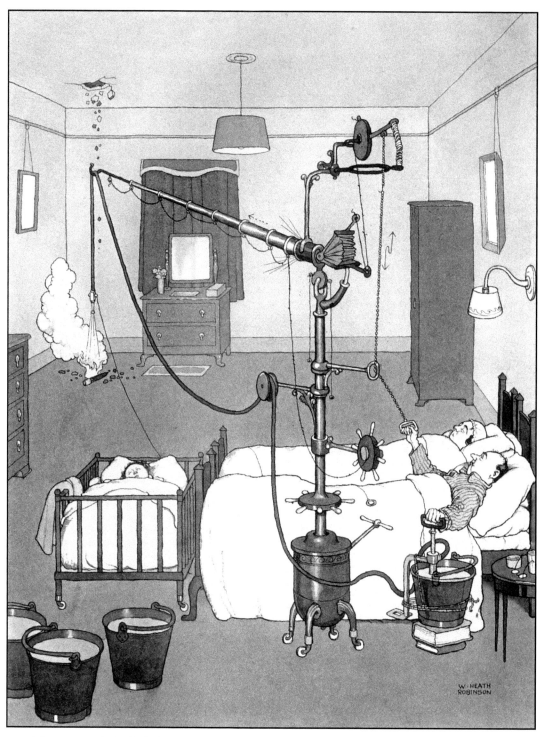

The ever-ready bedside bomb extinguisher.

Cooling buoys lowering the temperature of the Gulf Stream.

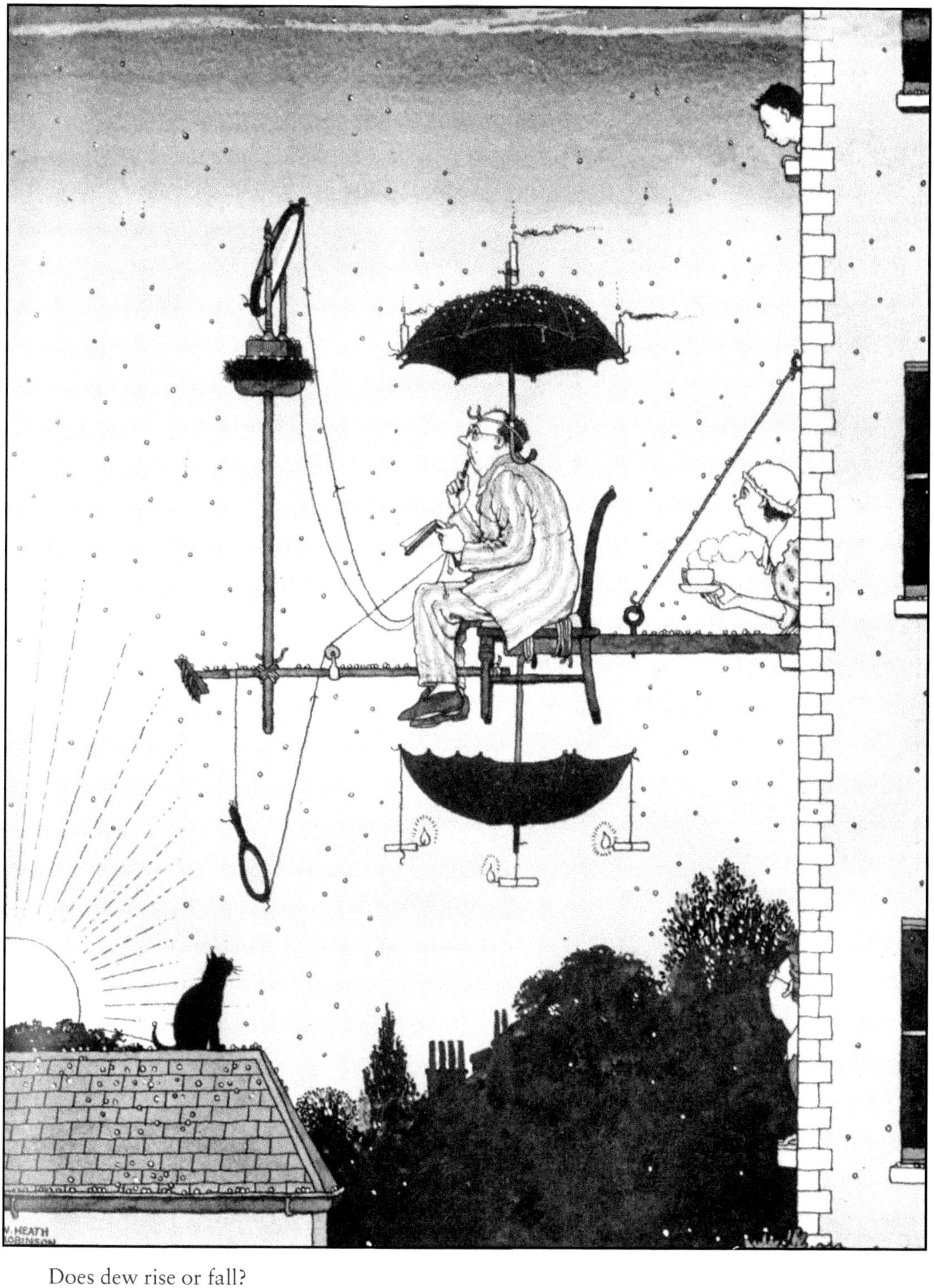
W. HEATH ROBINSON

Does dew rise or fall?

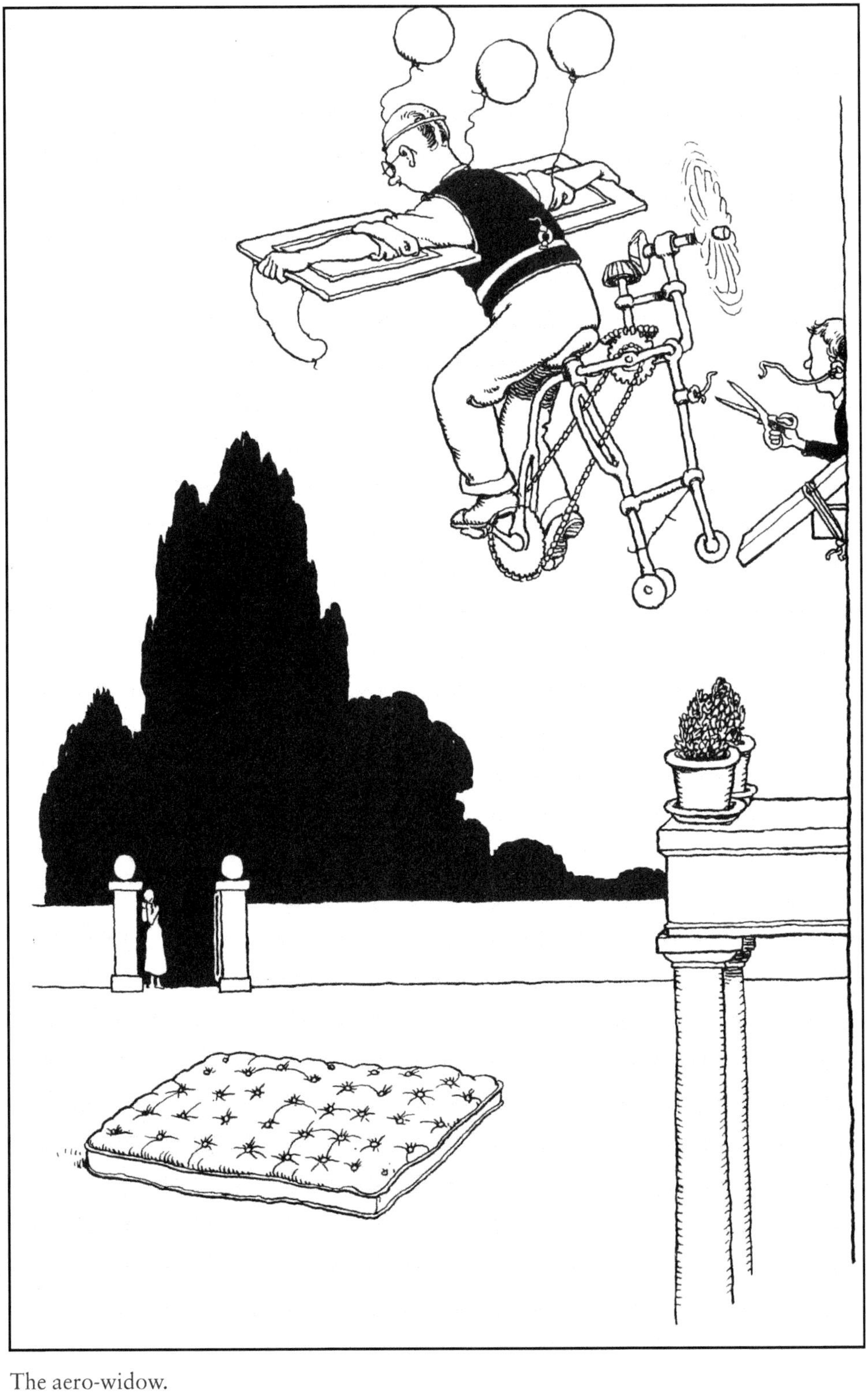

The aero-widow.

Candidates for water divining.

Taking one's own photo while bathing.

Tea and sugar rationing.

Automatic egg rationer.

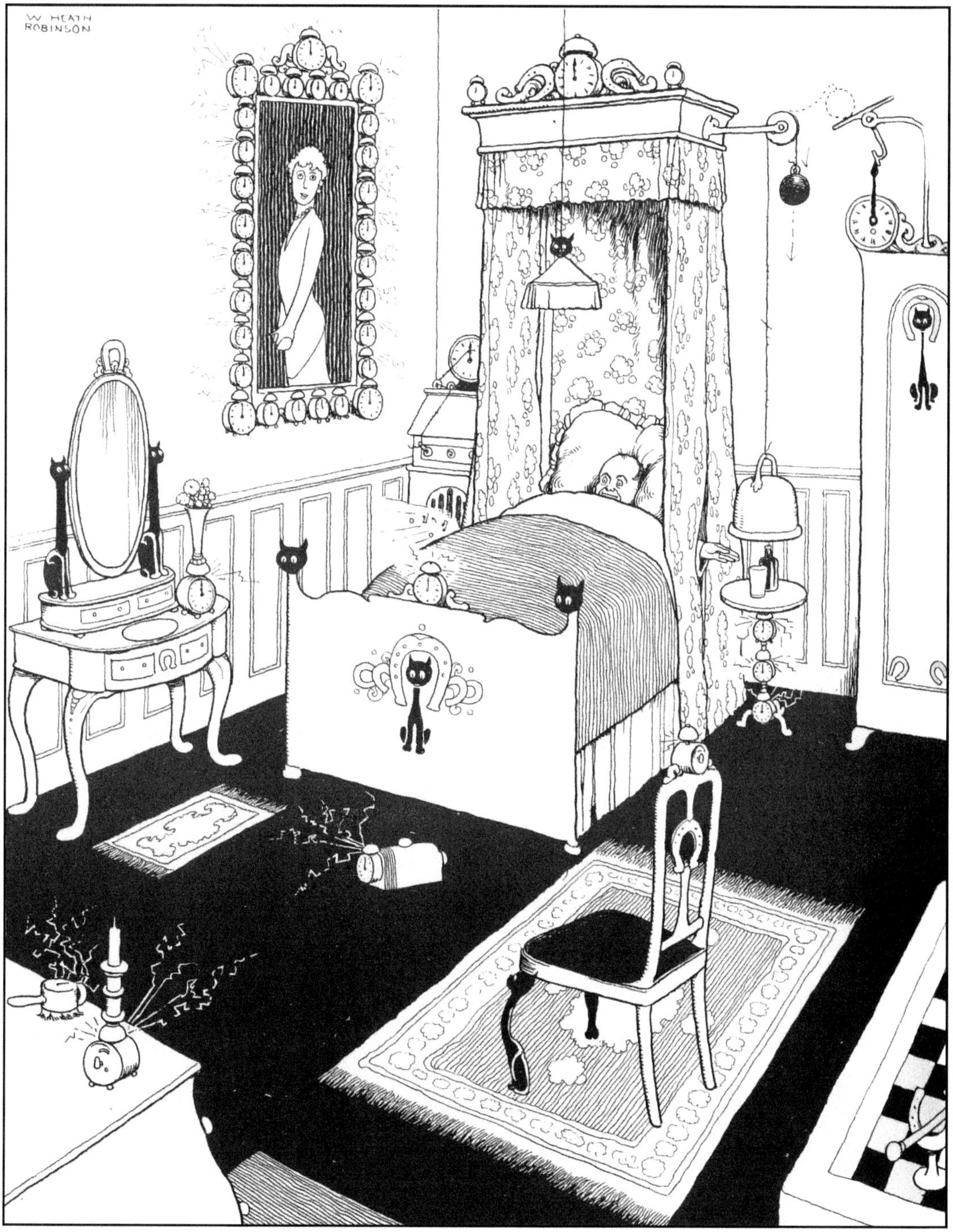
W. HEATH ROBINSON

Bedroom Suite de Luxe.